TABLE OF CONTENTS

INTRODUCTION

Kosovo…illuminates in many ways how America and our allies and adversaries are going to approach the art of war well into the next century.
— William S. Cohen, United States Secretary of Defense[1]

On 24 March 1999, the North Atlantic Treaty Organization (NATO) began its first war, a seventy-eight day military campaign against Serbia.[2] NATO conducted military action solely under alliance auspices, without a United Nations Security Council Resolution. Although the political and military end states for the campaign were not finalized until well into the campaign, NATO fought to compel Serbian President Slobodan Milosevic back to the bargaining table on the issue of Kosovo. NATO also aimed to put an end to the ethnic cleansing of Albanian Kosovars by Serbian forces in Kosovo, while simultaneously setting the conditions for Internally Displaced Personnel and refugees to return safely to their homes. To a lesser extent, NATO also fought to diminish the military capability of Serbian forces.

The 1999 war over Kosovo was part of the larger story of the disintegration of the former Yugoslavia. Throughout the 1990s, ethno-religious identity proved more powerful than the fragile political unity of the Yugoslav state. Ties to outside powers exacerbated tensions within the country. It also brought to the forefront, NATO's struggle for viability and purpose in the twenty first century. For NATO, continued conflict in Kosovo threatened to destabilize the entire Balkans with not only a surge of refugees but also the potential for violent confrontation along religious and ethnic lines.[3] With nearly an eighty percent Muslim population, fighting in Kosovo

---

[1]William S. Cohen, speech given to the International Institute for Strategic Studies, Hotel Del Coronado, San Diego, CA, 9 September 1999. http://www.defense.gov/speeches/speech.aspex?sppechid=470 (accessed 27 September 2012).

[2]Serbia will be used throughout the monograph to denote both Serbia and Federal Republic of Yugoslavia.

[3]The Contact Group, made up of four NATO nations (France, Italy, the United Kingdom, and the United States) and Russia, provided the diplomatic interface with Serbia throughout much

could very well spread to Albania and the Former Yugoslav Republic of Macedonia (FYROM), both of which have large Muslim populations. NATO perceived continued violence in Kosovo as having a direct negative effect on stability in Serbia, Bulgaria, and Greece.[4] Having just celebrated the end of the Cold War, NATO enlargement in Eastern Europe, and the re-emergence of the European Union, Europe could not tolerate ethnic cleansing in the Balkans.[5] Kosovo also tested the U.S.'s commitment to Europe through the NATO organization both politically and militarily. U.S. Ambassador Ivo Daalder summarized this struggle for an enduring role, in his April 2009 testimony to the U.S. Senate Foreign Relations Committee: "The key question for the United States now must be how we and our Allies can make NATO as effective in the 21st Century as it was in the 20th; how to make this Alliance, which has stood us so well for so long, an effective partnership to meet the challenges of today and tomorrow."[6]

The war in Bosnia, just a few years beforehand, shaped the expectations and conduct of military operations as many of the Allied senior leaders, both military and political, had dealt with a defiant Milosevic earlier in the 1990s during the war in Bosnia. Kosovo also highlighted the United States' lack of a comprehensive post-Cold War national strategy for the 21st century. Additionally, like many conflicts following the end of World War II, Kosovo quickly turned into an incremental, coercive war, which was substantially less than total warfare. The war also

---

of the crisis. Steve Bowman, *Kosovo: U.S. and Allied Military Operations*, CRS Report 1B10027 (Washington, DC: Office of Congressional Information and Publishing, 24 July 2000).

[4]Misha Glenny, *The Balkans: Nationalism, War and the Great Powers, 1804-1999* (New York: Penguin Books), 656.

[5]Paul E. Gallis, *Kosovo: Lessons Learned from Operation Allied Force,* CRS Report RL30374 (Washington, DC: Office of Congressional Information and Publishing, 19 November 1999).

[6]Ivo Daalder, statement to U.S. Senate Foreign Relations Committee, 22 April 2009, http://nato.usmission.gov/mission/ambassador.html (accessed 17 November 2012).

claimed the career of the victorious senior US military officer due to its divisive elements among U.S. political leadership and senior military officials.

In his 2003 book, *The Utility of Force: The Art of War in the Modern World*, General Sir Rupert Smith provocatively suggested, "war no longer exists…war as cognitively known to most non-combatants, war as battle in a field between men and machinery, war as a massive deciding event in a dispute in international affairs: such war no longer exists."[7] From this viewpoint, the last large scale and decisive tank battle involving supporting joint fires occurred in the 1973 Arab-Israeli war, making large armored tank formations and accompanying operations and tactics, no longer applicable in the current state of warfare.[8]

This monograph uses Smith's six characteristics of war to analyze the 1999 military campaign against Serbia.[9] It also explores the consequences resulting from the Allies' initial

---

[7]Rupert Smith, *The Utility of Force: the Art of War in the Modern World* (New York: Vintage, 2003), ix-xiii, 3. Having served a forty-year military career in the Army of the United Kingdom, General Sir Rupert Smith is well qualified to put forth theory on war having witnessed and thought about the topic from senior levels of leadership for the UK, NATO and the United Nations Protection Force (UNPROFOR). He has served and commanded during the Cold War, the first Gulf War, operations against the Irish Republican Army in Northern Ireland, Bosnia, Kosovo, Afghanistan and Iraq conflicts. General Smith began military service in 1962 and received his commission into the British Army in 1964. He commanded at senior levels not only with the British Defense force but also in NATO and the UN. In the first Gulf War, he commanded the British Armored Division, UNPROFOR in Bosnia in 1995, and as the NATO Deputy Supreme Allied Commander Europe (DSACUER) from 1998 to 2001 under United States Army (USA) General Wesley Clark, who served as SACUER during the 1999 Kosovo Campaign. During his NATO and UNPROFOR experience, General Smith commanded over 19 nations in each organization. He also served on senior staff positions in the United Kingdom as the Assistant Chief of Defense for two years following the first Gulf War, from 1992-1994. General Smith retired in 2002.

[8]Ibid., 4.

[9]Smith, *The Utility of Force: the Art of War in the Modern World,* 19-20. Smith's characteristics include: "1) The ends for which we fight are changing from the hard absolute objectives of industrial war to more malleable objectives; 2) We fight amongst the people, a fact amplified literally and figuratively by the central role of the media: we fight in every living room in the world; 3) Our conflicts tend to be timeless, since we are seeking a condition which then must be maintained until an agreement on a definitive outcome, which may take years or decades; 4) We fight so as not to lose the force, rather than fighting by using the force at any cost to

failure to heed General Smith's (ex post facto) warning regarding "a lack of coherence, whether in purpose or between purpose and force" as a failure to deliver a utility of force.[10] While this monograph explores the motives and actions of key NATO governments, it focuses primarily on the dynamics between senior U.S. political and military figures. The scope of the monograph includes brief information on the British role, primarily that of Prime Minister Tony Blair, as well as a brief synopsis of the Russian, German, French and Italian government positions throughout the conflict.[11] The monograph also uses statements and supporting facts from NATO, Serbian and Russian leadership, to support the concept of war among the people in Kosovo.[12]

While it may be several decades before all the relevant archival material is available, there is a sizeable literature of memoirs and secondary accounts pertinent to the 1999 Kosovo conflict. This monograph relies on English-language material. Notable memoirs include US President Bill Clinton's *My Life*, British Prime Minister Tony Blair's *A Journey*, Secretary of State Madeleine Albright's *Madam Secretary*, U.S. Chairman of the Joint Chiefs of Staff General Hugh Shelton's *Without Hesitation: The Odyssey of an American Warrior*, and, Supreme Allied Commander, Europe and Commander in Chief, European Command, U.S. General Wesley Clark's *Waging Modern War*.[13] Information from interviews or press conferences includes: U.S.: President William Clinton; Secretary of State Madeleine Albright; National Security Advisor

---

achieve the aim; 5) On each occasion new uses are found for old weapons; 6) The sides are mostly non-state since we tend to conduct our conflicts and confrontations in some form of multinational grouping."

[10]Ibid., 21.

[11]See Appendix 1 for a list of Key Personnel.

[12]See Appendix 2 for a map of Kosovo and Appendix 3 for NATO Command Structure and Key U.S. Military Leadership at Appendix 2.

[13]William J. Clinton, *My Life* (New York: Alfred A.Knopf, 2004); Tony Blair, *A Journey: My Political Life* (New York: A. Knopf, 2010); Madeleine Albright, *Madeleine Albright, Madam Secretary* (New York: Miramax Books, 2003); Henry H. Shelton, *Without Hesitation: The Odyssey of an American Warrior* (New York: St. Martin's Press, 2010); Wesley K. Clark, *Waging Modern War* (New York: Public Affairs, 2001).

Samuel "Sandy" Berger; (now) U.S. Ambassador Ivo Daalder; Secretary of Defense William Cohen; Assistant Secretary of Defense Kenneth Bacon; the Commander of Air Forces Southern Europe and 16th Air Force, U.S. Air Force Lieutenant General Michael Short; NATO: Secretary General Javier Solana; Supreme Allied Commander, Europe and Commander in Chief, European Command, U.S. Army General Wesley Clark; Chairman of the Military Committee, German General Klaus Naumann.

Key secondary sources address conflict in the Balkans and material written specifically about the NATO campaign against Serbia. Those that address conflict in the Balkans include Misha Glenny's *The Balkans*; Tim Judah's *Kosovo: War and Revenge*; Robert Kaplan's *Balkan Ghosts*; and R. Craig Nation's *War in the Balkans, 1991-2002*.[14] The military campaign against Serbia are discussed in Ivo Daalder and Michael O'Hanlon's *Winning Ugly*; Nardulli's *Disjointed War: Military Operations in Kosovo, 1999*; David Halberstram's *War in a Time of Peace: Bush, Clinton and the Generals*; Dag Henriksen's *NATO's Gamble: Combining Diplomacy and Airpower in the Kosovo Crisis 1998-1999*; and, Anthony Cordesman's *The Lessons and Non-Lessons of the Air and Missile Campaign in Kosovo*.[15] Finally, the monograph relies on reports

---

[14]Misha Glenny, *The Balkans: Nationalism, War and the Great Powers, 1804-1999* (New York: Penguin, 2001); Tim Judah, *Kosovo: War and Revenge* (New Haven: Yale University Press, 2000); Robert D. Kaplan, *Balkan Ghosts: A Journey Through History*(New York: St. Martin's Press, 1993); R. Craig Nation, *War in the Balkans, 1991-2002* (Carlisle Barracks, Carlisle, PA: Strategic Studies Institute, U.S. Army War College, August 2003).

[15]Ivo H. Daalder and Michael E., O'Hanlon, *Winning Ugly, NATO's War to Save Kosovo* (Washington, DC: Brookings Institution Press, 2000); Bruce R. Nardulli, et al., eds., *Disjointed War: Military Operations in Kosovo, 1999* (Santa Monica, CA: RAND, 2002); David Halberstam, *War in a Time of Peace: Bush, Clinton and the Generals* (New York: Scribner's, 2000); Dag Henriksen, *NATO's Gamble: Combining Diplomacy and Airpower in the Kosovo Crisis 1998-1999* (Annapolis, MD: Naval Institute Press, 2007); Anthony Cordesman, *The Lessons and Non-Lessons of the Air and Missile Campaign in Kosovo* (Westport, CT: Praeger, 2001).

from the U.S. Library of Congress Research Service and military after-action reports from the U.S. Department of Defense and the United Kingdom.[16]

THEORY OF WAR AMONGST THE PEOPLE

Following the end of World War II, the world has witnessed technologically advanced military forces soundly winning the majority of all battles at the tactical and operational level, yet losing at the strategic level of war. Modern warfare is not confined to only symmetric state on state conflict between military forces representing single nations. The nature, purpose, and goals of war have also changed in that seeking total surrender of a nation is rarely the goal of military action. Now more than ever, military action merely sets the conditions for a political end state— an end state negotiated by politicians and diplomats. Industrial war comprising of large armored formations, bombing of civilian populations by air forces, and decisive large-scale infantry battles, ended with the detonation of two atomic bombs on Japanese civilian populations in World War II.

Several authors have recognized this new type of warfare that emerged after World War II and have put forward different models and approaches to explain the change.[17] Having served forty years in the British Army, General Smith's six characteristics of post-World War II war

---

[16]United Kingdom General, Retired, Sir Rupert Smith, U.S. Ambassador Ivo Daalder, Permanent Representative on the Council of NATO since 2009; Michael O'Hanlon, now a senior fellow with the 21st Century Defense Initiative and director of research for the Foreign Policy program at the Brookings Institution; Misha Glenny, then the Central European correspondent for BBC World New Service; Bruce Nardulli, Walter Leo Perry, Bruce Pirnie, John McGinn and John Gordon IV, RAND Cooperation Senior Analysts; Lieutenant Colonel Dag Henriksen, Head of the Department for Air Power and Technology, Royal Norwegian Air Force Academy; Journalist David Halberstram, Pulitzer Prize winner for reporting in Viet Nam and runner up for his book used in this monograph.

[17]Many authors have recognized the change in war since the end of World War II. To name a few, Thomas C. Shelling's *Arms and Influence,* United Kingdom Field Marshall Sir Michael Carver's *War Since 1945*, United Kingdom General Sir Rupert Smith, *The Utility of Force: The Art of War in the Modern World*, and Everett Dolman, *Pure Strategy: Power and Principle in the Space and Information Age*.

under the auspice of war among the people, is a notable theory, worthy of further investigation. The six characteristics, found in varying degrees in each of the post-World War II conflicts, are strongly evident in the Kosovo campaign. The six characteristics suggest the character of war has changed. War among the people is the new paradigm of modern warfare. War is no longer about a single massive decisive battle where both the military and political objectives line up precisely. Instead, the six characteristics prevalent in war among the people, dominate the conflict, a conflict fought by the military to set the condition for political and diplomatic negotiations. War among the people is so different from industrial war, a true paradigm change has occurred. In Thomas Kuhn's explanation, the paradigm shift occurred because of the old paradigm's (industrial age warfare) inability to address military conflict and confrontation following the end of World War II.[18] The perceived anomalies of the industrial war model of conflict, fail to explain conflict following the end of World War II. Even in the case of the first Gulf War, although Iraqi forces were successfully expelled from Kuwait, the strategic end state left the leader of the country, his government, political party, and military and police forces in power to continue to serve as a counterweight to Iran's influence in the region. Similarly, post-Cold War conflict fought in Korea, Viet Nam, in the Balkans (Bosnia and Kosovo), Palestine and more recently, wars in Afghanistan (by the former Soviet Union and the United States) and the second Gulf War were fought for limited objectives short of total surrender.[19]

It is worth noting not all authors agree with General Smith's contention that industrial warfare is obsolete. Author Colin Gray recognizes that although there is a recent trend of conflict below large interstate warfare and total war, industrial warfare as witnessed earlier in the twentieth century is not dead. He disagrees with the basic assumptions and ambiguity over the

---

[18]Thomas S. Kuhn, *The Structure of Scientific Revolutions*, 3rd ed. (London and Chicago: University of Chicago Press, 1996), 84.

[19]Smith, *The Utility of Force*, 5.

definition of major states. Finally, he reemphasizes the narrative behind the "rise and fall of total war and second the decline and demise of major interstate war, is not to be trusted."[20] Although this author does not intend to dispute Colin Gray's claims, General Smith's theory on war among the people and the utility of force is a plausible theory for explaining conflict following the end of World War II.

According to Smith, war among the people "reflects the hard fact there is no secluded battlefield upon which armies engage, nor are there necessarily armies, definitely not on all sides."[21] War among the people is in fact fought where people live, where they work, and in their social settings. Civilians serve as targets in the sense that they must be won as one of the conditions for victory at the strategic level.[22] In contrast to industrial war's sequence of peace-crisis-war-resolution-peace, war among the people exhibits a "continuous crisscrossing between confrontation and conflict, regardless of whether a state is facing another state or a non-state actor."[23] Additionally, war among the people does not follow a sequence but can jump and skip an entire phase. Finally, although a particular conflict (Korea, Bosnia, Kosovo, Iraq, Afghanistan and Libya) ends militarily, the confrontation ultimately continues.

For industrial war, the sequence of confrontation is peace-crisis-war-resolution-peace. In other words, wars up to and including World War II, were fought and resolved, resulting in a new peace.[24] In addition, the sheer numbers of men and equipment coupled with a technological advantage over the enemy often proved decisive. Max Boot in his article, *The New American Way of War*, echoed author Russell Weigley's conclusions from his book titled *The American Way of*

---

[20]Colin S. Gray, *Another Bloody Century, Future Warfare* (Phoeniz, AZ: Orion Books, 2005), 138-139.

[21]Smith, *The Utility of Force*, 5.

[22]Ibid., 6.

[23]Ibid., 18.

[24]Ibid., 19.

War: A History of United States Military Strategy and Policy, with the following insight: "In this view, the Civil War, World War I, and World War II were not won by tactical or strategic brilliance but by the sheer weight of numbers—the awesome destructive power that only a fully mobilized and highly industrialized democracy can bring to bear…U.S. armies composed of citizen-soldiers suffered and inflicted massive casualties." [25] Industrial war is nation or state-on-state conflict, involving massed forces created through the efforts of the nations' industry and labor bases. [26] This idea is further supported by Clausewitz's paradoxical trinity model where he argues the people and their "primordial violence, hatred, and enmity;" the commander and his army with "chance and probability within which the creative spirit is free to roam" and finally, the government and its "element of subordination, as an instrument of policy" are in a balance, thus supporting the classic industrial war model. [27] However, this balance is usually not the case with war among the people.

The theory on the utility of force hinges on the two immediate effects of military force (composed of men, material, and logistics support) which is defined as killing people and destroying things. The measure of how killing people and destroying things achieves the overarching political purpose it was intended to achieve, measures the utility of military force. In order to maximize the utility of force, General Smith stated, "to apply force with utility implies an understanding of the context in which one is acting, a clear definition of the result to be achieved…and, as important as all others, an understanding of the nature of the force being

---

[25]Max Boot, "The New American Way of War," *Foreign Affairs* 82, no. 4 (July/August 2003): 41-58; Russell F. Weigley, *The American Way of War: A History of United States Strategy and Policy* (Bloomington, IN: Indiana University Press, 1973).

[26]Smith, *The Utility of Force,* 18.

[27]Carl Von Clausewitz, *On War*, ed. and trans. by Michael Howard and Peter Paret (Princeton, NJ: Princeton University Press, 1976), 89.

applied."[28] For initial operations in Kosovo, lack of a coherent political purpose wreaked havoc with NATO's military utility for the first half of the military campaign. A campaign that was expected to last only a few days by senior American and NATO officials dragged on for seventy-eight days.

MODERN WAR IN THE BALKANS

The following context for war in Kosovo illustrates General Smith's third characteristic of war among the people, namely, "conflicts tend to be timeless." Shifting demographics in Kosovo post-1960 facilitated ethnic tensions and Serbia's effort to fight any efforts toward Kosovo's independence. Demographically, the Kosovar Albanians were significantly altering the ethnic mix of the province. From 1948-1961, ethnic Albanians accounted for 67 percent of the population and Serbs accounted for 27.5 percent. By the 1980s however, the Albanian population grew steadily to account for 77 percent of the population while the Serb population dwindled to approximately 15 percent. Serb migration from the province coupled with significantly higher birth rates among Albanians accounted for the swing in population away from ethnic Serbs.[29] Over three quarters of Serbs who departed Kosovo cited violence, threats, and theft of possessions as the driving force behind their departure. This trend in the province of Kosovo, the heart of Serbia, did not sit well with Serb nationalists such as Milosevic who chose to use historical justification for including Kosovo in Serbia. Following the constitutional reforms in 1989, Milosevic purged Albanians from key positions in all of Kosovo and replaced them with Kosovar Serbs.[30]

---

[28]Smith, *The Utility of Force,* 3.

[29]Nebojsa Vladisavljevic, "Grassroots Groups, Milosevic or Dissident Intellectuals? A Controversy over the Orgins and Dynamics of the Mobilisation of Kosovo Serbs in the 1990s," *Nationalities Papers* 32, no. 4 (December 2004): 783.

[30]Ibid., 791.

Due to the shifts in demographics as well as Milosevic's actions, pluralism in Kosovo no longer existed. As a result, Kosovar Albanians now only dominated one demographic, the country's population.[31] The history of the Balkans and its relationship with Russia, Turkey (Ottoman Empire), Greece, Germany and Austro-Hungary beginning in the 7th century of the Common Era (C.E) also played a role in the lead up to the conflict.[32] Nonetheless, the proximate

---

[31]David Halberstam, *War in a Time of Peace: Bush, Clinton and the Generals* (New York: Scribner's, 2000), 364.

[32]According to the "Kosovo Country Review" published in 2012 by Country Watch, in the 7th century C. E. (common era), Serbs settled in what is now Serbia, Montenegro, Kosovo and Bosnia-Herzegovina. The first autonomous Serbian state was formed under Stefan I Nemanja (1159-1196). Under self-proclaimed emperor Stefan Dusan (1331-1355), the Serbs extended their reach from now modern day Belgrade to Greece. The Byzantine Empire sent the Turks to fight Serb forces in 1345 and 1345, with Serbs suffering defeat in 1352. Serbian Prince Lazar Hrebeljanovic fought the Turks again in the Battle of Kosovo Polje in 1389. Although he and the sultan were killed in battle, heroism, honor and the pride of Serbian people were celebrated an a national holiday on St. Vitus Day, June 28. In the 15th century, Turks conquered the last Serbian forces at Smederjevo in 1459, causing Serbs to flee to nearby countries of Hungary, Montenegro, Croatia, Dalmatia and Bosnia. For fifteen years beginning in 1684, Christian forces fought to expel Turks from the Balkans but failed. In 1718, Austrian forces took book Serb regions south of Sava from the Turks but the Jesuits who followed came to make the Serbs "hate the Austrians" as much as the Turks following their intense conversion efforts. Russia gained influence in the region in the 18th century when they were granted the "diplomatic right to protect Christian subjects of the Turks." Both Russia and Austria fought war against the Turks in 1787 and 1788 that was joined by Serbian forces who used guerilla tactics against the Turks. The Turks attached rebel Serb strongholds in 1813 alongside Bosnian and Albanian soldiers who ransacked Serbian villages, leading to a Serb uprising in 1815. The sultan recognized Serbia as a Turkish principality in 1830 and also reiterated Russia's right to protect Serbia. The treaties of San Stefano and Berlin in 1878 transformed Serbia into an independent state. Much to the frustration of the Serbs Austria-Hungary annexed Bosnia and Herzegovina in 1908. During the Balkan wars, the Serbs helped rid the Balkans of the Turks and won back land lost in the 13th and 14th century. Following the end of World War I, Serbian, Croatian and Slovenian leaders, "formed the federation known as Yugoslavia…later renamed as the Kingdom of Yugoslavia." Following the establishment of the kingdom, border disputes with Italy, Austria, Hungary, Bulgaria and Albania intensified disagreements with the Kingdom's neighbors, most notably Italy who did not receive all the land they thought they were entitled to in the 1915 Treaty of London. The creation of Yugoslavia combined together Serbs, Croats and Slovenes all of whom had their own separate convictions regarding government, culture and religion. Following German occupation in World War II, the socialist federation of Yugoslavia formed with Josip Broz Tito serving as the leader until 1980, when he passed away. Tito put in force a new constitution that recognized the "autonomous nature" of Kosovo with similar rights granted to the six republics of Yugoslavia (Serbia, Montenegro, Bosnia-Herzegovina, Croatia, Macedonia and Slovenia. In 1991-1992, several countries (Slovenia, Croatia and Bosnia-Herzegovina) left Yugoslavia via violent

cause of conflict in the Balkans in the 1990s was closely wrapped up in the personalities and process of Yugoslavia's disintegration.

Under the rule of wartime resistance leader Marshal Josip Broz Tito, Yugoslavia maintained a relatively stable existence through much of the Cold War. After Tito's death, long-standing internal tensions in Yugoslav society began to manifest themselves. In 1989, Milosevic stripped away Kosovo's autonomy granted by Tito in 1974.[33] Tito, half Slovene and half Croat, served as Supreme Executive Officer, Head of the Armed Forces and finally President of the Socialist Federal Republic of Yugoslavia from 1953 until his death in May 1980.[34] Although Tito championed national reconciliation in the Balkans, his successors proved more willing to champion ethno-religious particularisms. Author R. Craig Nation points out, "the war of Yugoslav Succession was essentially a civil war, with fellow citizens set at one another's throats at the behest of ruthless and unprincipled leaders engaged in a struggle for power and dominion."[35]

In June of 1989, President Slobodan Milosevic rallied Serbians around nationalism and the sacred place Kosovo played in the history of the Balkans, specifically to Serbia. He cited the battle of the Balkans in 1389, known as the Battle of Kosovo Field, to stir national pride.[36] Milosevic portrayed Muslims as aiding the Turkish forces in this battle, thus contributing directly

---

measures while Macedonia was also able to do so though peacefully. Yugoslavia, Serbia and Montenegro adopted the constitution of the Federal Republic of Yugoslavia on April 17, 1992 (11-15). For a thorough review of the history of conflict in the Balkans, see Misha Glenny's, *The Balkans: Nationalism, War, and the Great Powers, 1804-1999*, and the aforementioned Kosovo Country Review.

[33]Daalder and O'Hanlon, *Winning Ugly, NATO's War to Save Kosovo,* 78.

[34]Richard Cavendish, "Tito Elected President of the Former Republic of Yugoslavia," *History Today* 53, no. 1 (June 2003): 56.

[35]R. Craig Nation, *War in the Balkans, 1991-2002* (Carlisle, PA: Strategic Studies Institute, 2003), x.

[36]Ivo H. Daalder and Michael E., O'Hanlon, *Winning Ugly, NATO's War to Save Kosovo* (Washington, DC: Brookings Institution Press, 2000), 78.

to a thorough Serbian defeat. In one particular speech on 29 June 1989, celebrating the new

Serbian constitution as well as the 600th Anniversary of the Battle of Kosovo Field, Milosevic

used emotional rhetoric to glorify the Serbian forces that fought.[37] He stated the cause of the loss

for Serbia was due to internal divisions and disunity in Serbia. Milosevic later remarked the

disunity no longer exists in Kosovo. Television and radio stations transmitted the speech live

across much of Serbia and repeated it numerous times throughout the day. Although the Serbs

were handily defeated in the Battle of Kosovo Field, Milosevic's message was unmistakable: he

would personally restore Serbia's national pride and identity.[38]

According to Misha Glenny, after the Dayton Peace Accords negotiations, it was clear to

Kosovar Albanians that peaceful resistance to the Serbian government would not gain the West's

attention and support for independence.[39] In fact, according to the Kosovo Country Review, "the

Kosovo province was treated as part of Serbia in the new successor state—Federal Republic of

Yugoslavia."[40] Only armed conflict would move the West to do something as only those who

fought and shed blood in Bosnia gained respect and recognition during the Dayton Peace

Accords.[41] Kosovar Albanians saw Bosnia gain independence following the war as well as $5

---

[37]Agneza Bozic Roberson, "The Role of Rhetoric in the Politicization of Ethnicity: Milosevic and the Yugoslav Ethnopolitical Conflict," *Razprve in Gradivo - Treaties & Documents*, 52 (2007): 277.

[38]Ibid., 278.

[39]Glenny, *The Balkans: Nationalism, War and the Great Powers, 1804-1999*, 653-654. On 14 December 1995, "the Dayton Peace Accords were signed in Paris, France, ending three and half years of violent and bloody war in Bosnia and Herzegovina, the most brutal conflict in Europe since the Second World War. The accords led to the deployment of NATO's first peacekeeping force to oversee implementation of the military annex of the peace agreement. This was an important milestone, not only for security in the Western Balkans, but also for NATO's post-Cold War transformation." North Atlantic Treaty Organization Web page, http://www.nato.int/cps/en/natolive/news_69290.htm (accessed April 8, 2013).

[40]Kosovo Country Review, Country Watch, Inc., http://connection.ebscohost.com 2012, (accessed 27 January 2013).

[41]Halberstam, *War in a Time of Peace: Bush, Clinton and the Generals,* 366.

billion pledged from the international community to rebuild Bosnia-Herzegovina.[42] Just five

months after the peace accords for Bosnia, the Kosovo Liberation Army (KLA) began its

offensive against the Kosovar Serb population and authority with an attack on Serbs at a café in

Decani, in western Kosovo. Following the attack in the café, which killed three Serbs, three more

attacks on Serbs occurred in the next hour. With the first act of violence in Decani, the KLA

commenced its armed resistance against the Serbian government as many more attacks against

the Serb population and authority in Kosovo continued throughout the duration of the conflict.[43]

In November 1997, at a funeral for a KLA member, a KLA soldier made a speech,

lighting the spark for the conflict and popularizing the KLA and their cause: "Serbia is

massacring Albanians…The KLA is the only force that is fighting for the liberation and the

national unity of Kosovo. We shall continue to fight!" to which the crowd chanted "KLA, KLA,

KLA"[44] In mid-December 1997, the international community began to take note of the escalating

violence in Kosovo, perpetrated by both the KLA and Serbian regular military and police forces.

The North Atlantic Council (NAC) issued a statement of "profound concern," condemning both

Albanian violent repression at the hands of Serb forces and terrorist acts committed by the KLA

against the Serb population and its police forces.[45] Increasing concern and warnings from the

NAC, other senior NATO officials, the United Nations, and the international community

---

[42]Glenny, *The Balkans: Nationalism, War and the Great Powers, 1804-1999*, 653.

[43]Ibid., 652.

[44]Tim Judah, *Kosovo: War and Revenge* (New Haven: Yale University Press, 2000), 130-131.

[45]According to NATO's webpage, "the North Atlantic Council is the principal political decision-making body within NATO. It brings together high-level representatives of each member country to discuss policy or operational questions requiring collective decisions. In sum, it provides a forum for wide-ranging consultation between members on all issues affecting their peace and security." North Atlantic Treaty Organization Weg page, http://www.nato.int/cps/en/natolive/topics_49763.htm (accessed November 28, 2012); Bruce R. Nardulli, Walter L Perry, Brice Prinie, John Gordon IV, John G. McGinn, *Disjointed War: Military Operations in Kosovo, 1999* (Santa Monica, CA: RAND), 13.

continued up until the beginning of NATO's air campaign. On several occasions, NATO

Secretary Javier Solana publically blamed President Milosevic for the violence in Kosovo. Unlike

the war in Bosnia where Milosevic relied on local Serb surrogates, in Kosovo, he directly

oversaw and controlled the level of violence.[46] United Nations Security Council Resolution 1160,

issued in March 1998, condemned excessive use of force by Serbian units against Kosovar

civilians and imposed an arms embargo on Serbia and Montenegro.[47]

Key Leaders and Governments

This section primarily focuses on political leadership in the United States (President of

the United States ((POTUS)), Secretary of State, Secretary of Defense and SACEUR) and briefly

touches on NATO Secretary General Javier Solana, British Prime Minister Tony Blair and the

governments of Russia, France, Germany, Italy, and Greece. Some members of President

Clinton's national security team are also addressed.[48] Limits of space prevent an exhaustive

---

[46]Daalder and O'Hanlon, vii.

[47]Bruce R. Nardulli, et al., eds., *Disjointed War: Military Operations in Kosovo, 1999* (Santa Monica, CA: RAND, 2002), 13.

[48]For an overview of President Clinton's National Security Council, see David J. Rothkopf, *Running the World: The Inside Story of the National Security Council and the Architects of American Power* (New York: Public Affairs, 2005), 344-88. Clinton Presidential Records Mandatory Declassification Review, An Administrative marker used by the William J. Clinton Presidential Library Staff, 200 pages. Although the Clinton Administration was distracted over the Lewinsky affair, according to declassified summaries from the President's National Security Council Deputies Committee Meeting, the issue of the Balkans and conflict in Kosovo was discussed multiple times per month. Earliest records available from the released material began in June 1998 where Kosovo was a primary topic of discussion. Although attendance varied depending on the topics, primary attendees for discussions regarding Kosovo included: Vice President's Office: Leon Fuerth, Leslie Davidson; Departments of State: Secretary Madeleine Albright, Strobe Talbott, Richard Holbrooke (later as Special Envoy); Defense: William Cohen; Joint Chiefs of Staff: Generals Hugh Shelton or Joseph Ralston and Gen George Casey; National Security Advisor and Chair: Samuel Richard "Sandy" Berger; Central Intelligence Agency: George Tenet, the National Security Council: Jock Covey; U.S. Ambassador to the United Nations: William Richardson, Nancy Soderberg; U.S. Ambassador to the North Atlantic Treaty Organization: Alexander "Sandy" Vershbow   Due to the limited amount of material in his autobiography, this monograph will not address Chairman of the Joint Chiefs of Staff, General

review of all those in Europe and the United States who participated in the planning and execution of Operation ALLIED FORCE.

In the United States, President William Clinton was halfway through the second term of his presidency.[49] Relations between the President and the military institution began poorly and according to author Dale Herspring, "would be characterized more by conflict than cooperation from the day he entered office, although it would improve slightly over time."[50] As a result, both sides tended to avoid the tough, complex problems and instead talked around them. This gave the perception that tension between senior military officials and the White House administration was very high, which in fact was the case.[51] Clinton also faced a somewhat hostile Congress, controlled by the Republican Party. Congress was also uninterested in the prospects of bombing

---

Hugh Shelton's impact on the campaign.   In the Chairman of the Joint Chiefs of Staff biography, *Without Hesitation, The Odyssey of an American Warrior* (with Ronald Levinson and Malcolm McConnell) (New York: St. Martin's Griffin, 2010), GEN Shelton mentions Kosovo on 6 pages of his 524 page book. Although he attended (directly or through representation via the VCJCS or JCS J-5) all NSC discussions regarding Kosovo, the NSC meetings were mandatory, whereas mentioning Kosovo in his own personal memoir was left to his discretion.

[49]In his autobiography, *My Life* (New York: Alfred A. Knopf, 2004), reflects the killings in Kosovo reminded him of Bosnia with Kosovo serving as the bridge between, "European Muslims and Serb Orthodox Christians, a dividing line along which there had been conflict from time to time for six hundred years" (849). He also adds that he was determined to let "Kosovo to become another Bosnia. So Was Madeleine Albright." Clinton also noted the complexity of relations with Russia following their notification regarding a NATO attack on Serbia. On March 23, 1999, Vice President Al Gore informed Russian Prime Minister Yevgeny Primakov regarding NATO's impending military action. The prime minister, who was on his way to the United States on an airplane to see Gore, had his airplane turn around and head back to Russia (850). He also gives two reasons for forgoing an initial ground campaign with U. S. troops. First, it would take too long to build up adequate troop numbers to protect civilians from ethnic cleansing; second, the civilian casualties from a ground campaign would be too great (851). At the end of March, Clinton acknowledged Tony Blair was ready to send in ground troops, a move Clinton had hoped to delay until the mission changed to peacekeeping (852). In his 957-page autobiography slightly more than twenty pages mention Kosovo with half of those detailing his thoughts and understanding of the situation.

[50]Dale R. Herspring, *The Pentagon and the Presidency* (Wichita, KS: University Press of Kansas, 2005), 332.

[51]Halberstam, *War in a Time of Peace: Bush, Clinton and the Generals,* 411.

in Kosovo for fear of what might follow, should a bombing campaign fail to coerce Milosevic.[52]

In addition, a month prior to NATO military action in Kosovo, the President of the United States

had narrowly survived an impeachment attempt following an affair with White House intern

Monica Lewinsky. Clinton had avoided impeachment but at the expense of attention in other

matters, most notably the Balkans and foreign affairs in general.[53]

Secretary of State Madeleine Albright was more than willing to fill the void and provide

her thoughts regarding foreign policy to resolve conflict in Kosovo.[54] In a statement to the Senate

Foreign Relations Committee in April 1999, she stated:

> By opposing Slobodan Milosevic's murderous rampage, NATO is playing its rightful role
> as a defender of freedom and security within the Euro-Atlantic region. Because our cause
> is just, we are united. And because we are united, we are confident that in this
> confrontation between barbaric killing and necessary force; between vicious intolerance
> and respect for human rights; between tyranny and democracy; we will prevail.[55]

Secretary Albright's family history and her experience while serving in the United

Nations during the war in Bosnia shaped her beliefs and honed her resolve on Kosovo,

specifically with Milosevic.[56] In her commencement address to Harvard graduates on 5 June

1997, she stated: "We have a responsibility...not to be prisoners of history, but to shape

---

[52]Ibid., 387.

[53]Daalder and O'Hanlon, *Winning Ugly, NATO's War to Save Kosovo*, 2.

[54]Herspring, *NATO's Gamble: Combining Diplomacy and Airpower in the Kosovo Crisis 1998-1999*, 364-365. In her autobiography, *Madam Secretary, Madeleine Albright*, a substantial amount of pages is spent discussing war in the Balkans, the most of all individual leaders that are reviewed in this monograph.

[55]Madeleine Albright, Secretary of State, "U.S. and NATO Policy Toward the Crisis in Kosovo," statement before the Senate Foriegn Relations Committee, 20 April 1999, http://www2.lhric.org/validation/war/articles/albright.html (accessed 19 November 2012).

[56]Jeremy Byman, *Madam Secretary: The Story of Madeleine Albright* (Greensboro, NC: Morgan Reynolds Inc, 2008), http://connection.ebscohost.com 2012, Combined Arms Research Library Internet Site (accessed 26 September 2012). Albright was born in Czechoslovakia on May 15, 1937. In that year, the Nazi's threatened the relatively new country and finally in 1939, arrived to occupy and repress it. Just ten days later, her family, a Jewish family, narrowly escaped Czechoslovakia for London, England.

history...and to build with others a global network of purpose and law that will protect our citizens, defend our interests, preserve our values, and bequeath to future generations a legacy as proud as the one we honor today."[57] According to Ivo Daalder and Michael O'Hanlon, Albright, "forcefully took the lead in devising an appropriate response to end the violence."[58] She preferred the six-nation Contact Group as her means to develop an acceptable approach to Kosovo. One year prior to the commencement of NATO military operations against Serbia, Secretary Albright made her intentions clear with the following statement in Rome at the Ministry of Foreign Affairs: "We are not going to stand by and watch Serb authorities do in Kosovo what they can no longer get away with in Bosnia."[59] Consistent with General Smith's sixth characteristic for war among the people, NATO, a conglomeration of numerous nations, would serve as the international community's vehicle to take action against Serbia. [60]

William S. Cohen served as U.S. Secretary of Defense from 1997-2001. He was born in Bangor, Maine, in 1940 and later served as both a Representative and Senator from that same state. He graduated from Boston University Law School, and served as Chairman for the Select Committee on Indian Affairs and a Special Committee on Aging, prior to his selection for U.S.

---

[57]Ibid.

[58]Daalder and O'Hanlon, *Winning Ugly, NATO's War to Save Kosovo,* 25.

[59]NATO leadership initially formed the Contact Group in response to the crisis in Bosnia. It consisted of members from the United States, United Kingdom, France, Italy and Russia. Eventually the Contact Group worked to restore autonomy to Kosovo instead of independence from Yugoslavia, as was desired by Kosovar Albanians. CRS Issue Brief for Congress, *Kosovo: U. S and Allied Military Operations* (24 Jul 2000, CRS-2); Secretary of State Madeleine Albright, "Press Briefing at the Ministry of Foreign Affairs," Rome: U.S. Department of State, March 7, 1998.

[60]Rupert Smith, *The Utility of Force: the Art of War in the Modern World,* 21. The sixth characteristic for war among the people stated by General Smith is as follows: "The sides are mostly non-state since we tend to conduct our conflicts and confrontations in some form of multinational grouping whether it is an alliance or a coalition, and against some party or parties that are not states."

Secretary of Defense by Clinton in 1997.[61] In a PBS Frontline Interview, when asked what the

U.S. should do regarding involvement in Kosovo, Cohen responded with an answer in the spirit

of the Powell Weinberger doctrine:

> I felt that military force should be the absolute last resort. Everything else has to fail
> before you turn to the military. And if you do turn to the military, you must be very clear
> on what the objectives are, measuring those political objectives, and how military action
> can be consistent with carrying out and furthering those goals. I want to be very clear that
> we have domestic support before we ever commit our forces to combat... Also, we must
> have the support of the allies.[62]

Another interesting aspect of Cohen's service was his relationship with senior U.S. military

figures and General Wesley Clark's perception regarding his premature replacement and

subsequent early retirement.[63]

General Clark, no stranger to conflict with Serbian President Slobodan Milosevic, also

greatly shaped the NATO response for Kosovo. A few years earlier, General Clark played a key

role in the Dayton Accords as the Joint Chiefs of Staff Director of J-5 for Strategic Plans and

Policy. In this position, he worked directly with the Clinton Administration, most notably,

---

[61]Biographical Directory of the United States Congress, William S. Cohen, http://bioguide.congress.gov/scripts/biodisplay.pl?index=C000598 (accessed 29 January 2013).

[62]Michael A. Cohen, "The Powell Doctrine's Enduring Relevance," *World Politics Review* (22 July 2009), http://www.worldpoliticsreview.com/articles/4100/the-powell-doctrines-enduring-relevance (accessed 29 January 2013); Interview with William Cohen, PBS Frontline, n.d., http://www.pbs.org/wgbh/pages/ frontline/shows/kosovo/interviews/cohen.html (accessed 29 January 2013). The Powell-Weinberger Doctrine states the following conditions should be considered by policy makers prior to committing U.S. forces: "1) The United States should not commit forces to combat overseas unless the particular engagement or occasion is deemed vital to our national interest or that of our allies.; 2) If we decide it is necessary to put combat troops into a given situation, we should do so wholeheartedly, and with the clear intention of winning; 3) If we do decide to commit forces to combat overseas, we should have clearly defined political and military objectives; 4) The relationship between our objectives and the forces we have committed —their size, composition and disposition—must be continually reassessed and adjusted if necessary; 5) Before the U.S. commits combat forces abroad, there must be some reasonable assurance we will have the support of the American people and their elected representatives in Congress; 6) The commitment of U.S. forces to combat should be a last resort."

[63]On the relationship between Secretary Cohen and General Clark, see Clark's book titled, *Waging Modern War*, 408-12.

Assistant Secretary Richard Holbrooke. For the impending conflict in Kosovo, Clark was dual-hatted as the Supreme Allied Command of European Forces (SACEUR) and Commander in Chief, United States European Command (CINCEUR).[64] His dual chains of command dictated he work for NATO Secretary General Javier Solana while simultaneously answering to William Cohen, U.S. Secretary of Defense (SECDEF). He also needed to maintain close contact with both the General Hugh Shelton, USA, Chairman of the Joint Chiefs of Staff and General Dennis Reimer, U.S. Army Chief of Staff. His position was difficult to navigate given the Department of Defense's (DOD) reluctance to take action in Kosovo.[65] After having a conversation with GEN Shelton on June 1, 1999, Clark subsequently wrote, "As I listened to him, I realized that I had little idea, and never had during the entire crisis, how the Commander in Chief or the Secretary of Defense were making decisions. Wouldn't they have been able to make better decisions, and have them better implemented, I thought, if they brought the commander into the high-level discussions occasionally?"[66] This was a chilling insight into relationships with civil and military leadership in the DC beltway and their warfighting commander dual hatted as SACEUR and CINCEUR.

Bradley Graham, a Washington Post writer, quoted a senior military officer familiar with deliberations in the "tank" leading up to the campaign in Kosovo, "I don't think anybody felt like there had been a compelling argument made that all of this was in our national interest."[67] However, both Clark and Albright, having been involved in direct diplomacy with Milosevic to

---

[64]General Clark served as the Supreme Allied Commander of European Forces and Commander in Chief, United States European Command from July 11, 1997 to May 3, 2000.

[65]Herspring, *The Pentagon and the Presidency,* 363.

[66]Wesley K. Clark, *Waging Modern War* (New York: Public Affairs, 2001), 341.

[67]Bradley T. Graham, "Joint Chiefs Doubted Air Strategy," *Washington Post*, 5 April 1999. The "tank" is one of the secure conference rooms used by the Chairman of the Joint Chiefs of Staff.

conclude the war in Bosnia, firmly believed a serious credible threat of military force must underpin any diplomacy that aimed to resolve conflict in Kosovo.[68] DOD's stubborn reluctance against U.S. military action in Kosovo, coupled with General Clark and Secretary Albright's determination to use force, most likely led to Clark's early replacement as SACEUR and subsequent early retirement from the U.S. Army.[69]

NATO Secretary General Javier Solana was focused on keeping NATO together during the conflicts in the Balkans (both in Bosnia and Kosovo) as well as putting an end to the ethnic violence while maintaining stability in the region.[70] Linda Kozaryn quoted Solana saying the following:

> All efforts to achieve a negotiated political solution to the Kosovo crisis having failed, no alternative is open but to take military action...We must halt the violence and bring an end to the humanitarian catastrophe now unfolding in Kosovo...NATO's goal is to prevent further human suffering and repression and violence against the civilian population of Kosovo.[71]

Further, Solana was determined that, "NATO will do whatever is necessary to bring stability to the region," and that NATO, "must stop an authoritarian regime from repressing its people. We have a moral duty to do so. The responsibility is on our shoulders and we will fulfill it."[72] Solana acknowledged NATO's expanded role of intervention in another country's sovereignty, "We're

---

[68]Herspring, *The Pentagon and the Presidency*, 362.

[69]David Stout, "U.S. General Who Led NATO to Retire Ahead of Schedule," *New York Times*, 28 July 1999, http://connection.ebscohost.com 2012 (accessed 27 September 12).

[70]According to NATO's internet site (http://www.nato.int/cv/secgen/solana.htm, accessed 27 January 2013), Solana was born in Madrid, Spain in 1942 and served as a professor of Physics and was also a member of the Spanish Parliament from 1977-1995. Next, he served as NATO Secretary General beginning in December 1995 just as NATO deployed the multinational Implementation Force (IRFOR) to the Bosnia to enforce agreements made in the Dayton peace accords. He served as Secretary General through 1999.

[71]Linda D. Kozaryn, "NATO Orders Air Strikes to End Humanitarian Catastrophe" *Armed Forces Press Service*, 24 March 1999, http://www.defense.gov/News/NewsArticle.aspx?ID=42000 (accessed 28 January 2013.

[72]Ibid.

moving into a system of international relations in which human rights, rights of minorities every

day, are much more important. More important even than sovereignty."[73] General Clark clearly

saw Solana as determined to, "save NATO's reputation in the region and its credibility."[74]

British Prime Minister Tony Blair's contribution toward NATO efforts in Kosovo had

significant impact for Operation ALLIED FORCE as a strong proponent for military force and

the use of ground troops.[75] According to a CRS Report, "Among governments strongly

supportive of Allied Force, the perception is common that British Prime Minister Tony Blair's

government, not the Clinton Administration, provided the key political leadership."[76] An

"influential strategist" in the U.K. noted that although the U.S. was providing the preponderance

of combat capability in Kosovo, "America does not have the same interests in the outcome of a

European war as those living in the region."[77]

Among other key Allied governments, the French government was a strong supporter for

campaign objectives. The military campaign made French President Jacques Chirac re-think

---

[73]James Kitfield, "Not so Sacred Borders," *PBS Frontline*, 2000, http://www.pbs.org/wgbh/pages/frontline/shows/kosovo/procon/kitfield.html, (accessed 28 January 2013.

[74]Clark, *Waging Modern War*, 134.

[75]Tony Blair, *A Journey, My Political Life* (New York: Borzoi Book, 2010). Former British Prime Minister Tony Blair devotes an entire chapter of his autobiography to Kosovo. On the atrocities going on in Kosovo, Blair notes, "This was ethnic cleansing. What's more, it was happening right on Europe's border…from the onset, I was extraordinarily forward in advocating a military solution," which, "put a colossal strain on my personal relationship with Bill Clinton" (226-227). Blair saw a need to do something in Kosovo as a moral issue and a great disappointment that Milosevic carried out the atrocities on Europe's doorstep in the 1990s (228). In early 1999, he worked on the American and European leadership and gained their concurrence to condemn Milosevic's action but he was unsuccessful in gaining their support for ground troops. For Blair, he saw the lack of willingness to commit ground troops in January 1999 as an "utterly hopeless negotiating tactic with Milosevic. It signaled from the outset that there was a limit to our seriousness of intent, and that provided he could withstand the air campaign, he could survive" (230).

[76]Paul E. Gallis, *Kosovo: Lessons Learned from Operation Allied Force*, RL30374 (Washington, DC: Office of the Congressional Information and Publishing, 19 November 1999).

[77]Ibid., 20.

France's relationship with NATO and the prerequisite of having a U.N. mandate prior to the use of force, something the French government had previously insisted on. German government officials from the beginning and throughout did not support the use of ground forces against Serbia. German Chancellor Gerhard Schroeder's central concern was stemming the flow of refugees and putting a quick end to the ethnic cleansing in Kosovo. Germany's aircraft strike sorties were the first flown since World War II. The Italian government led by President Oscar Scalfaro, was initially conflicted over participation in ALLIED FORCE. However, the Italian government did provide key airspace and airfield access for strike aircraft. Given Italy's close proximity to the Balkans, it took a critical role in caring for refugees in Albania and Macedonia. Finally, although Greek Prime Minister Konstantinos Simitis endorsed NATO's objectives, he was also quick to note his concern that war in Kosovo could cause border issues for the Balkans and destabilize the region.[78]

Leading up to military conflict, Russia President Boris Yeltsin's government did not support the threat of NATO bombing in Serbia, arguing the situation should be settled diplomatically. Russia also noted the events in Kosovo occurred within the sovereign territory of Serbia. According to Russian Foreign Minister Igor Ivanov, Serbia was dealing with the problem of "the breeding ground for Islamic extremism."[79] Russia, a member of the Contact Group on Yugoslavia and a veto-holding member in the United Nations, supported peace negotiations in Rambouillet, France in 1999. The Yeltsin government supported several U.N. Security Council Resolutions (1160, 1199 and 1203) that created an arms embargo against Serbia as well as calling

---

[78]Ibid., 20-21.

[79]Jim Nichol, *Kosovo Conflict: Russian Responses and Implications for the United States*, CRS-1 (Washington, DC: Office of Congressional Information and Publishing, June 2, 1999). Report for Congress, 2 June 1999, CRS-1.

on Serbia to cease ethnic cleansing in Kosovo.[80] However, when military operations commenced against Serbia, the Russians reacted with "great shock" in response to NATO's "naked aggression." Ivanov stated NATO leaders should be tried by the international war crimes tribunal for the air strikes which caused "genocide" in Serbia.[81] Russians perceived the airstrikes as highlighting their overall weakness and power decline in Asia and Europe. Hardline and ultranationalists used the NATO military campaign as proof that NATO enlargement was a direct threat to Russian, which also served to undermine Yeltsin's authority.[82]

On the Road to War

In April 1998, General Clark directed Admiral James Ellis, U.S. Navy, Commander of Allied Forces Southern Europe, to determine preventative deployment plans to enter Albania and Macedonia to help provide stability along the borders of Yugoslavia. Per request from the North Atlantic Council, the Military Committee also looked into the, "full range of graduated options to deter further violence and to influence the behavior of the parties to the conflict."[83] The task for the Military Committee was two-fold: consider requirements to support peace operations and the requirements for a land and air offensive capability. President Clinton's October 1998 statement indicated a limit to America's commitment in the Balkans, "I don't think the American people will support U.S. ground troops in Kosovo."[84] According to authors Nardelli and Pirnie, by the summer of 1998 "forced-entry ground operations were effectively ruled out by both senior NATO political authorities and U.S. political and senior military advisors."[85] From that point on, NATO

---

[80]Ibid., CRS-1.

[81]Ibid., CRS-2.

[82]Ibid., CRS-3-4.

[83]Nardulli, et al., *Disjointed War: Military Operations in Kosovo*, 14.

[84]Ibid., 15.

[85]Ibid., 14.

did not plan for any type of ground operations. This early decision essentially ceded the initiative to Milosevic. It also sent a strong signal to him regarding NATO's weak resolve to push Serb forces out of Kosovo.[86] Almost a year prior to actual military combat against Serbia, the alliance settled on air power by process of elimination, as the sole military tool aimed to force Milosevic to comply with diplomatic efforts for a peace settlement in Kosovo.

The decision to settle on airpower was not a simple decision but a result of "having to do something in Kosovo," coupled with the distaste for the use of ground forces. Remarkably, aside from NATO officials, few observers actually believed air power would force Milosevic back to negotiations. Some military experts view airpower as the ultimate instrument of military coercion.[87] Typically, air power advocates portray air power as clean and surgical due to its historical low threat of friendly casualties and enemy collateral damage. The last thing NATO wanted was to be perceived as "acting inhumanely" while carrying out a military campaign to halt repression and ethnic cleansing in Kosovo.[88] NATO was also reluctant to destroy key infrastructure in Serbia, not to mention the will of the Serbian people, since the prospects of Serbia joining the European Union was a definite possibility. No European country had the desire to pay a huge reconstruction bill associated with rebuilding a totally defeated and broken Serbia.[89] With the exception of Tony Blair's government, the appetite for using ground forces in Kosovo was non-existent in the international community. The final choice faced by political leaders was

---

[86]Ibid., xiv.

[87]Michael Clarke, "Airpower, Force and Coercion," *The Dynamics of Airpower* (1996). In his article, Michael Clarke does not specify which NATO officials believed bombing would coerce Milosevic back to negotiations.

[88]Nardulli, et al., *Disjointed War: Military Operations in Kosovo*, 27.

[89]Ibid., 33-34.

to "do nothing" or use air power.[90] For Kosovo, NATO initially failed to undertake a coherent use of military action employed to achieve a political objective to ensure the utility of military force.

In October 1988, Holbrooke and Short met with Milosevic and reached concessions regarding a three pronged Kosovo Verification Mission (KVM) aimed to ease tensions.[91] Although the verification missions did not stop the escalation of violence, it did lead the West to believe Milosevic would once again, just like in Bosnia, back down when threatened with aerial bombardment. After the massacre of forty-five ethnic Albanians in the town of Racak by Serbian security forces, which occurred on 15 January 1999, the NAC again threatened the use of airpower on 30 January 1999.

On 6 February 1999, the Rambouillet Conference began as a last ditch diplomatic effort to avoid military conflict. After the conference, Sandy Berger stated if Milosevic "was playing a game with us at Rambouillet by building up his force while pretending to negotiate, so were we. We needed to demonstrate a real commitment to get a peaceful resolution in order to get the allies to go along with the use of significant force."[92] One of Albright's close aides put the purpose of the conference in clearer terms, stating it was held to "get the war started with the Europeans locked in."[93] The main failure of the conference related to NATO's inclusion of its prerogative to insert forces in greater Serbia, not just Kosovo. Milosevic made it clear from the very beginning this was a non-starter. Upon further review, much of the Rambouillet Conference draft agreement

---

[90]Steve Bowman, *Kosovo: U.S. and Allied Military Operations*, CRS Issue Brief for Congress (Washington, DC: Office of Congressional Information and Publishing, 24 July 2000), 4.

[91]Henriksen, *NATO's Gamble: Combining Diplomacy and Airpower in the Kosovo Crisis 1998-1999,* 153-154; Short concluded from his conversations with Milosevic, "If you hit that man hard, slapped him upside the head, he'd pay attention" (153).

[92]Daalder and O'Hanlon, *Winning Ugly, NATO's War to Save Kosovo,* 89.

[93]Joseph Fitchett, "Main Winner: U.S. Support for EU," *International Herald Tribune* (11 June 1999): 1.

was "borrowed" from the Dayton Peace Accords agreement, which included this same clause.[94]

In the Dayton Peace Accords however, the clause related to Croatia and allowed NATO forces to enter Croatia. NATO forces in Serbia, however, were a very different matter. In terms of establishing peace, the Rambouillet Conference failed to reach its goal of having both sides agree to the terms of the settlement.[95] The U.S. was successful in demonstrating diplomacy would not work with Milosevic. The conference also secured the support of NATO for military action in Kosovo. On 19 February 1999, even before the Rambouillet Conference ended, the NATO Secretary General threatened the use of airstrikes to avoid a human catastrophe in Kosovo.[96]

Another noteworthy fact during the conflict is the U.N. had not endorsed NATO's action against Serbia. NATO officials knew China and Russia would not pass a U.N. measure supporting the use of military force against Serbia.[97] By proceeding forward without the resolution, NATO demonstrated it would not be constrained by U.N. politics.[98] Although a weak argument, NATO did have implied authority under the United Nation's Charter Chapter VII and therefore did not ignore the United Nations. In Chapter VII, Article 42 in the 23 September 1998 United Nations Security Resolution, which permits "it (the Security Council) may take such action by air, sea, or land forces as may be necessary to maintain or restore international peace and security. Such action may include demonstrations, blockade, and other operations by air, sea,

---

[94]Daalder and O'Hanlon, *Winning Ugly, NATO's War to Save Kosovo*, 87.

[95]Only the Kosovar Albanian delegation finally agreed to sign the accords on 18 March 1999.

[96]Nardulli, et al., *Disjointed War: Military Operations in Kosovo, 1999*, 17-18.

[97]In early October 1998 at a Contact Group meeting in London, Russian Foreign Minister Ivanov told the British, French and German foreign ministers who wanted to pursue a United Nations Security Council Resolution for the use of force is Kosovo, "If you take it to the UN, we'll veto it." He went on further to say, "if you don't [take it to the U.N] we'll just make a lot of noise…saying it was all foreshadowed, The Russians can't do anything. NATO is the power." Henriksen, *NATO's Gamble: Combining Diplomacy and Airpower in the Kosovo Crisis 1998-1999*, 152.

[98]Bowman, *Kosovo: U.S. and Allied Military Operations*, 2.

or land forces of Members of the United Nations."[99] Former Swedish Prime Minister Ingvar

Carlson's comments represent those world leaders who did not agree with the previous

assessment of U.N. legitimacy: "NATO air strikes against Yugoslavia have not been authorized

by the U.N…They are therefore acts of aggression against a sovereign nation. They strike at the

heart of the rule of international law and the authority of the U.N."[100] For NATO, proceeding

without a formal U.N. resolution to do so served as an exception.[101] General Smith justified the

Kosovo situation based on morality. To prevent ethnic cleansing and the repression of the

Kosovar Albanians, it was moral, even without clear U.N. approval, to make war on Serbia.[102] As

illustrated with Smith's logic, the reasons why we fight wars have changed. In this instance, to

save the ethnic Albanians, external forces would intervene in a sovereign state's internal affairs

for humanitarian reasons. [103]

Senior leaders in the U.S. and NATO believed the air war in Kosovo would be short with

Milosevic capitulating once he realized the Allies were serious, as witnessed by their willingness

to bomb Serbia. Then Lieutenant General Michael Short, USAF Commander Air Forces Southern

Europe and U.S. 16th Air Force stated, "I can't tell you how many times the instruction I got was

'Mike, you're only going to be allowed to bomb two, maybe three nights…That's all the alliance

can stand. That's why you've only got ninety targets. This will be over in three nights."[104]

---

[99]Charter of the United Nations, http://www.un.org/en/documents/charter/chapter7.shtml, (accessed 30 September 2012).

[100]Ingvar Carlson and Shridath Ramphal, "NATO's Vigilante Warfare gives a Bad Example to the World," *International Herald Tribune*, 1 April 1999.

[101]Stanley R. Sloan, "Continuity or Change? The view from America," *NATO After Fifty Years,* Victor S. Papacosma, Sean Kay, and Mark R. Rubin, eds. (Wilmington, DE: Scholarly Resources, 2001), 18.

[102]Smith, *The Utility of Force: the Art of War in the Modern World*, 390.

[103]Glenny, *The Balkans: Nationalism, War and the Great Powers, 1804-1999*, 660.

[104]Lt Gen Michael Short, USAF, interview by PBS Frontline (22 February 2000).

Leaders in the West operated on the assumption of the previous success of the air war in Bosnia and Holbrooke's negotiated concessions from Milosevic in the fall of 1998 after having threatened air strikes.[105]

Following the collapse of negotiations at the Rambouillet Conference and Holbrooke's failed last-ditch efforts to salvage peace directly with Milosevic just days before military operations commenced, NATO Secretary General Javier Solana directed General Clark to begin airstrikes. He cited Yugoslavia's refusal to accept the interim Rambouillet peace agreement, failure of the Kosovo Verification Mission and Serbia's continuous use of excessive force against Albanian Kosovars.[106]

Strategy and Planning

It was a strategy designed to somehow convince somebody that we were committed to something we were not committed to do.[107]

The political ends for which nations and military alliances fight, is changing. Due to constraints in key NATO countries, Kosovo never had the potential to be a high intensity conflict. Additionally, the Serbs knew they risked losing their military capability if they chose to challenge NATO military power might head-on. Instead, the Allies fought to achieve a condition whereby negotiations would resume. Regardless, peace would be something solved in diplomatic channels, as no NATO nation desired an outright military defeat of Serbia. The characteristic of fighting "so as not lose the force," greatly shaped every aspect and detail of the Allied plan from overall strategic objectives to the tactical level rules of engagement for NATO pilots.

---

[105]Dag Henriksen, *NATO's Gamble: Combining Diplomacy and Airpower in the Kosovo Crisis 1998-1999* (Annapolis, MD: Naval Institute Press, 2007), x.

[106]Nardulli, et al., *Disjointed War: Military Operations in Kosovo, 1999*, 18.

[107]Ivo Daalder, interview by PBS Frontline (n.d.).

The overall lack of a long-term plan to address Kosovo's struggle for independence is one of the most noted shortcomings among authors. Daalder and O'Hanlon wrote that NATO "had hope but not a plan. NATO stumbled into war, unready either for countering Serbia's massive campaign to forcefully expel much of the ethnic Albanian population from Kosovo or to do militarily what it would take to achieve its stated objectives."[108] General Clark's observations reflect the same perception and prove even more alarming given his position as SACEUR for the duration of the conflict as he notes, "there simply was no detailed planning. There was no strategic consensus in Washington. Even if there had been, U.S.-only planning would have been unrealistic since we never had any intention of fighting alone."[109] A British Defense Committee report places the blame squarely on the shoulders of the North Atlantic Council for failure "to reach an early consensus on its policy on recourse to military means, and the inhibitions within NATO on military contingency planning."[110] The lack of planning also manifested itself in the late decision to name the military operation, which did not occur until 23 March, one day prior to the 78-day air campaign. Washington initiated the impetus to determine the name for the campaign with a phone call to SACEUR.[111]

For SACEUR and his staff, given the lack of detailed planning prior to the initiation of bombing, General Clark had hoped once the operation had begun, he would have a few days to formulate a campaign plan. However, the media applied pressure and did not allow Clark to have several days to formulate the plan.[112] For Clark and the alliance, NATO military actions in

---

[108]Daalder and O'Hanlon, *Winning Ugly, NATO's War to Save Kosovo,* 18.

[109]Clark, *Waging Modern War*, 439-440.

[110]The Defence Committee, *Fourteenth Report. Report to Parliament* (London: Her Majesty's Stationery Office, 1999), Annex A Summary.

[111]Henriksen, *NATO's Gamble: Combining Diplomacy and Airpower in the Kosovo Crisis 1998-1999,* 6.

[112]Clark, *Waging Modern War,* 6-7, 188.

Kosovo were closely scrutinized by the press, a battle truly "fought among the people." General

Smith's second characteristic for war among the people states the role of the media plays a central

role in shaping military action as, "we fight in every living room in the world as well as on the

streets and field of a conflict zone."[113] Early on, General Clark acknowledged the significance of

the media's role in the campaign when we stated, "The media and press were going to be vitally

important." Clearly, Clark understood he had to provide the *jus ad bellum* for war in Kosovo and

maintain support from the international community through the media.[114]

Alliance Cohesion and Casualty Aversion

For the duration of the campaign, alliance cohesion was an overarching objective for the

NATO Secretary General and his organization. However, military action in Kosovo and the

Balkans challenged NATO's resolve from day one of the campaign. General Clark stated alliance

cohesion as one of his "measures of merit" for the campaign. The measure aimed to, "retain

alliance solidarity and the full support of our regional partners."[115] Clark's desire to maintain

alliance cohesion shaped all aspects of follow-on planning and execution for NATO. After all,

this was a NATO action and many of the nations, including the U.S., were reluctant to conduct

military operations for malleable objectives consistent with war among the people. From the

beginning, NATO countries found it difficult to connect a direct national threat to their interests

with the fighting that was going on in Kosovo.

Another top priority for senior NATO officials was to minimize NATO casualties or any

catastrophic civilian casualties. Senior alliance officials feared such an event could immediately

---

[113]Smith, *The Utility of Force: the Art of War in the Modern World*, 21.

[114]Clark, *Waging Modern War*, 188.

[115]Ibid., 184.

halt military operations prior to the condition being set for a political agreement. [116] General Clark sensed once the bombing started, a halt for reasons other than for the attainment of the NATO objectives, would prove disastrous. He believed the momentum to move NATO toward the resumption of bombing would be insurmountable.

The consequences for valuing alliance cohesion as the top priority trickled down to every level of planning and subsequent execution. For fear of failure, politicians in NATO nations became involved with the most detailed planning, to include the selection of individual air targets. Even with target selection however, NATO's lack of an overall plan negatively affected the process and diminished the utility of targets selected to achieve the end states. A British report stated this fact more somberly: "Despite the involvement of politicians, the selection of some strategic targets was politically ill-considered."[117] The tortuous process was similar to the U.S. Air Force's experience in the Rolling Thunder campaign in Viet Nam, where President Lyndon Johnson and his administration, "dictated the size of the striking force, its weapons, and the precise time of the attack."[118]

With alliance cohesion as the overarching objectives for the campaign early on, senior NATO military leadership developed three principles. General Klaus Naumann stated, "we had first of all to avoid if possible any of our own casualties and fatalities, secondly we were told to avoid collateral damage…and thirdly bring it to a quick end," which made it "very difficult to

---

[116]Nardulli, et al., *Disjointed War: Military Operations in Kosovo, 1999,* xiv, 46.

[117]The Defence Committee, Fourteenth Report. Report to Parliament, Point 301. http://www.parliament.the-stationery-office.co.uk/pa/ cm199900/cmselect/cmdfence /347/34702.htm (accessed 21 June 2012).

[118]Dennis Drew, "Rolling Thunder 1965: Anatomy of a Failure," Air University, School of Advanced Airpower Studies, Air University Press, October 1986. http://www.au.af.mil/au/awc/awcgate/readings/drew2.htm (accessed 9 March 2013).

find a proper solution."[119] Author Eliot Cohen captures the paradox of General Smith's "fight so as not to lose the force," noting the goals of fighting a military campaign while simultaneously avoiding casualties. He goes on to note it reflects an unwillingness and overall lack of understanding regarding the intended use of force and its utility toward achieving an end state.[120] The rules of engagement regarding the operating altitude for aircraft was one of the many manifestations of this paradox. Aircraft subordinated to the Close Air Support (CAS) mission, were not allowed to operate below 15,000 feet Above Ground Level (AGL) until the Commander, Allied Air Forces Southern Europe, or his designated representative, approved the pilot to drop weapons. Only after the approval would the CAS aircraft switch to the tactical air controller to employ bombs and fly below 15,000 feet AGL.[121] On a dynamic battlefield fought with small enemy units and equipment, this process often proved too lengthy for the application of timely military force.

American senior political leaders committed the gravest of errors regarding the development of a realistic military strategy for Kosovo. As early as October 1998, Sandy Berger confessed, "I don't think that the American people will support ground troops, U.S. ground troops in Kosovo."[122] Although the U.S. National Security Advisor made the statement to placate the U.S. public and Congress, Berger should have understood this statement would do more damage

---

[119]NATO Homepage, http://www.nato.int/cv/milcom/nauman-e.htm (accessed 28 January 2013); Klaus Naumann, interview by PBS Frontline 2000. According to NATO's homepage, German General Klaus Naumann served as the Chairman of the NATO Military Committee from 1996-1999. Naumann was born in Munich, Germany in 1939 and joined the German Army in 1958. He served tours in the German Ministry of Defense, Representative to the NATO Military Committee and then as the Chief of Military Policy, Nuclear Strategy and Arms Control Section.

[120]Eliot A. Cohen, *Soldiers, Statesmen, and Leadership in Wartime: Supreme Command* (New York: Anchor Books, 2003), 203.

[121]Nardulli, et al., *Disjointed War: Military Operations in Kosovo, 1999*, 34.

[122]Jeffrey R. Smith, "Accord on Kosovo Remains Elusive," *Washington Post* (12 October 1998).

to the perception of NATO's commitment than benefit. Additionally, Milosevic took this and follow-on statements as a lack of U.S. resolve and weakness. In the opinion of author Eliot Cohen, the rhetoric of "fighting so as not to lose the force," had the President himself as the author. Cohen believed Clinton was unable to reconcile the use of force and as a result, acted to minimize any chance for U.S. casualties.[123]

In fact, even when the military campaign began, President Clinton had not fully committed the efforts of the nation for military operations in Kosovo.[124] The night the campaign commenced, he inserted one line into his address to the nation saying, "I do not intend to put our troops in Kosovo to fight a war."[125] Clinton advisors would later admit this might have been a "considerable mistake," while senior military officials "thought it was, in fact, a catastrophic mistake because it sent the wrong signal to all kinds of people, most notably Slobodan Milosevic." [126] On 27 March, just three days into the campaign, Kenneth Bacon, Assistant Secretary of Defense for Public Affairs, continued the rhetoric of America's efforts to fight so as not to lose the force: "The United States has no intention of sending ground troops to fight in Kosovo, and the Department of Defense is not doing any planning that would enable such a deployment."[127] Several days later on 31 March, the President spoke about his rationale behind the "no troops on the ground" policy. In an interview with Dan Rather, he said, "the thing that bothers me about introducing ground troops into a hostile situation—into Kosovo and the

---

[123]Cohen, *Soldiers, Statesmen, and Leadership in Wartime: Supreme Command*, 203.

[124]It is the author's opinion, when a nation commits to military operations, it should do so fully prepared to consider all possible military capabilities or at the very least, not to rule them out. For Kosovo, President Clinton, to the detriment of the campaign, ruled out ground options even before the military campaign began.

[125]Halberstam, *War in a Time of Peace: Bush, Clinton and the Generals*, 423.

[126]Ibid., 423.9

[127]Department of Defense, "News Briefing," statement by Kenneth Bacon, Assistant Secretary of Defense for Public Affairs, (Washington, DC: 27 March 1999).

Balkans—is the prospect of never being able to get them out."[128] A few months later, Sandy

Berger, believed Congress would not approve funds for the operations unless the administration

acknowledged there was no intention of sending ground troops.[129] Regardless of the real impetus

behind the statement, it potentially could have made the military campaign shorter had the

President assured Congress of this intent behind closed doors. The litany of public statements

made it clear to NATO and Milosevic, the U.S. was not open to the use of all military

capabilities.

The lack of commitment by the U.S. was subsequently shared by NATO and could be

partially explained by the international community's expectation the campaign would be short.

Authors Daalder and O'Hanlon remarked, "Operation ALLIED FORCE was in its early weeks a

textbook case of how not to wage a war. The blindness of NATO's major members to the

possibility that the war might not end quickly was astounding."[130] Instead of a quick end to the

military campaign, Belgrade dug in and met the alliance's air campaign by adapting tactics,

preventing NATO from destroying Serbia's integrated air defense system. In fact, Milosevic

accelerated the ethnic cleansing of Albanians in Kosovo when the campaign began.[131] The West's

experience and lessons learned in Bosnia erroneously shaped the approach to Kosovo as the air

campaign in Bosnia had brought a quick settlement with Milosevic.[132]

Regardless of NATO expectations, the alliance was woefully unprepared for military

operations as it failed to produce a coherent strategy with clear end states. This was evident by the

---

[128]William J. Clinton, interviewed by Dan Rather, Columbia Broadcasting System, 31 March 1999.

[129]Daalder and O'Hanlon, *Winning Ugly, NATO's War to Save Kosovo,* 97; Nardulli, et al., *Disjointed War: Military Operations in Kosovo, 1999,* 23.

[130]Daalder and O'Hanlon, *Winning Ugly, NATO's War to Save Kosovo,* 19.

[131]Nardulli, et al., *Disjointed War: Military Operations in Kosovo, 1999,* 21.

[132]Klaus Naumann, interviewed by PBS Frontline, 2000.

number of aircraft and sustainment elements, or lack thereof, deployed in the region.[133]

Consistent with General Sir Rupert Smith's "fight so as not to lose the force," NATO had committed only 350 aircraft to the AOR when the bombing campaign began. The number of aircraft was about one third of the final aircraft that would end up fighting in Kosovo and only a tenth of the air power used against Iraq in the first Gulf War. Additionally, no aircraft carrier was available in the region at the beginning of military operations.[134]

The deployment of U.S. Army Apache helicopters to the Balkans is the ultimate example of the West's efforts to "fight so as not lose the force." Initially mentioned by General Hugh Shelton, Chairman of the Joint Chiefs of Staff to General Clark, the idea was to deploy 24 AH-64 Apache gunships to fight in coordination with the Multiple Launch Rocket System (MLRS) and fixed wing assets.[135] Military planners thought the Apache-MLRS capability would fill the gap left by fast-flying aircraft that could not engage small units of Yugoslav ground forces operating with little or no equipment in support. Additionally, military leaders believed gunships would force the Serb equipment out into the open, forcing it to reposition for survival or to engage the gunships directly. This would allow fixed wing assets to engage and destroy Serbia's larger equipment, something the West was largely unable to accomplish during the campaign. On 29 March 2009, the Army, Air Force and Marines non-concurred on Gen Clark's request to deploy the Apaches to Macedonia.[136] Although the U.S. deployed the Apaches and supporting equipment to the AOR although they were never employed for fear of losing them in combat.[137] In fact,

---

[133] Anthony Cordesman, *The Lessons and Non-Lessons of the Air and Missile Campaign in Kosovo* (Westport, CT: Praeger, 2001), 18-20.

[134] Halberstam, *War in a Time of Peace: Bush, Clinton and the Generals*, 444.

[135] Ibid., 464; Nardulli, et al., *Disjointed War: Military Operations in Kosovo, 1999*, 57.

[136] Ibid., 59.

[137] For more information regarding Task Force HAWK, see *Disjointed War: Military Operations in Kosovo, 1999* by Bruce R. Nardulli, et al, pages 57-91.

President Clinton never authorized the employment order because Service Chiefs predicted a high loss rate for the gunship. In a *Washington Post* article, writer Dana Priest provided a stark condemnation of the U.S.'s efforts to "fight so as not to lose the force:" "the vaunted helicopters came to symbolize everything wrong with the army as it enters into the 21st century…its obsession with casualties; its post-Cold War identity crisis."[138]

As the campaign increased pressure on Milosevic, General Clark requested and received more combat power in the form of more strike and supporting aircraft. U.S. Air Force Lieutenant General Michael Short wanted to destroy multiple strategic targets in the FRY simultaneously, specifically focusing on targets within the city of Belgrade. He wanted to apply all air combat power decisively and bring Milosevic to his knees in the shortest timeframe possible. Short believed fixed targets made sense since NATO, "could not stop the killing in Kosovo from the air…we were not going to be efficient or effective."[139] Short also believed General Clark never put forward his plan to hit Milosevic with everything the alliance had, a plan the Air Force designed to simultaneously neutralize all strategic targets in Serbia. In General Short's opinion, campaign execution was, "essentially toothless and squandered and neutered this remarkable (air power) technology."[140] However, General Clark understood the limitations associated with war among the people. Although not specifically stated, Clark understood the approach for Kosovo would have to be incremental, leaving room for negotiations to occur at any time in the campaign. Had NATO destroyed all targets during the first few days of the conflict without Milosevic surrendering, the results would have been disastrous for the alliance. General Clark also

---

[138]Dana Priest, "Army's Apache Helicopter Rendered Impotent in Kosovo" *Washington Post* (29 December 1999).

[139]Nardulli, et al., *Disjointed War: Military Operations in Kosovo, 1999,* 34; General Michael E. Ryan, (USAF), *The Air War over Serbia,* (Ramstein Air Force Base, Germany: Studies and Analysis Directorate, United States Air Force in Europe, 2000).

[140]Halberstam, *War in a Time of Peace: Bush, Clinton and the Generals,* 445.

understood maintaining the alliance was critical and he worried heavy bombing at the beginning of the campaign would have shattered alliance resolve and cohesion. Additionally, he was concerned with the international community perceiving him as the "butcher of Belgrade."[141] General Clark viewed Milosevic's ground forces in Kosovo as the center of gravity because they executed Belgrade's strategy to cleanse ethnic Albanians. Hence, destroying Serb ground forces was one of General Clark's top priorities.[142] General Short disagreed with Clark on his assessment of the Serb ground forces as a center of gravity. Eventually, Clark ordered Short to execute more air strikes on the forward ground units operating in Kosovo.[143]

Campaign Goals and End States

With the stage set for action against Serbia, NATO Secretary General Javier Solana, the U.S., and other Allied leaders declared the main thrust of military action was to end the ethnic cleansing in Kosovo and to enforce the interim agreement Milosevic had refused to sign.[144] On 23 March 1999, Solana announced NATO was taking action to enforce, "Acceptance of the interim political settlement which has been negotiated at Rambouillet; full observance of limits on the Serb Army and Special Police Forces agreed on 25 October 1998; ending of excessive and

---

[141]Ibid., 450.

[142]Clark, *Waging Modern War* and Nardulli, et al., *Disjointed War: Military Operations in Kosovo, 1999*, 33.

[143]Nardulli, et al., *Disjointed War: Military Operations in Kosovo, 1999*, xvi.

[144]NATO, "Political and Military Objectives of NATO Action with Regard to the Crisis in Kosovo," *NATO Information,* 23 March 1999, http://www.nato.inf/docu.pr.1999/p99-043e.htm (accessed 21 June 2012); Department of Defense, "News Briefing," statement by Kenneth Bacon, Assistant Secretary of Defense for Public Affairs, Washington DC, 23 March 1999.

disproportionate use of force in Kosovo."[145] Solana also added the action would prevent

instability from rippling through the entire Balkans.

In the United States, President Clinton announced NATO strikes had three objectives,

which were not fully consistent with statements by Solana just a day prior. In his television

address to the American people on 24 March, the President stated the goals of the campaign were

to, "demonstrate the seriousness of NATO's opposition to aggression and its support for peace.

Second, to deter President Milosevic from continuing and escalating his attack on helpless

civilians by imposing a price for the attacks. Third, if necessary, to damage Yugoslavia's capacity

to wage war against Kosovo."[146] Following the end of the war, a DoD lessons learned report for

Kosovo stated the POTUS objectives as NATO's strategic end states for Kosovo, demonstrating

that even after the fact, the overall strategy was not consistent at the very highest levels of

alliance leadership.[147] Given General Smith's discussion on the inability to link a military strategy

to political aims in Kosovo, it is no surprise the goals of the campaign were not consistent

between NATO and the U.S.

On 23 March 1999, SACEUR identified what he called his measures of merit for the

campaign over Kosovo: "the first...is not to lose aircraft, minimize loss of aircraft...second...is

to impact the Yugoslavia military and police activities on the ground as rapidly and effectively as

possible...third...is to protect our ground forces—and in this case SFOR, the elements of the

---

[145]Javier Solana, Secretary General of NATO, "Press Release (1999) 040," *NATO Information,* 23 March 1999, http://www.nato.inf/docu.pr.1999/p99-040e.htm (accessed 21 June 2012).

[146]William Jefferson Clinton, President, "Address to the Nation on Airstrikes Against Serbian Targets in the Federal Republic of Yugoslavia (Serbia and Montenegro)," Washington, DC, 24 March 1999, http://www.presidency.ucsb.edu/ws/?pid=57305.

[147]Department of Defense, "Kosovo/Operation Allied Force Report After-Action Report to Congress," (Washington, DC: Government Printing Office, 31 January 2000), xvii.

international community."[148] The stated military strategy from the NATO Secretary General,

POTUS and SACEUR consistently illustrated the emphasis on fighting so as not to lose the force.

General Clark also asked critical questions of his 4-star Generals regarding the effectiveness of

the campaign in regards to his measures of merit.[149] After nine days of the air campaign, Clark

asked his 4-stars during a VTC, "were we meeting our military objectives? How were these

linked to the political objectives? What were the political objectives? What is the end state?

When could we reach it?"[150] His measures of merit and assessments would help him shape a

successful strategy for NATO as the campaign went on.

With respect to the three NATO objectives, the alliance achieved limited results although

Milosevic eventually capitulated after a seventy-eight day campaign. In fact, when Operation

ALLIED FORCE began, the Serbs stepped up their efforts to cleanse ethnic Albanians. Given the

limited amount of air assets initially deployed and the restrictive rules of engagement, NATO had

neither the mass nor procedures in place to neutralize Serb military units operating on the

ground.[151] Simultaneously, the number of Serb forces on the ground more than tripled during the

conflict as Milosevic moved to hold out against the alliance while increasing efforts to cleanse

Kosovo. His Integrated Air Defenses (IADs) operated only sporadically, frustrating NATO

efforts to neutralize the system. The inability to destroy Serb IADs kept NATO pilots above

15,000 AGL unless cleared to fly at lower altitudes. The altitude restriction made timely and

efficient interdiction of enemy forces challenging. As a result, Serb forces on the ground had the

advantage and quickly developed tactics to operate in small units with minimal heavy equipment

---

[148]Clark, *Waging Modern War,* 183.

[149]In Clark's book, *Waging Modern War*, he does not specifically mention which 4-star generals he discussed the measures of merit with in regards to the air campaign over Kosovo.

[150]Ibid., 233.

[151]Nardulli, et al., *Disjointed War: Military Operations in Kosovo, 1999,* 49.

in support. In fact, since the spring of 1998, many Serb commanders already had experience operating in small units in Kosovo, giving them an advantage when NATO's air campaign began roughly a year later.[152] When the goal is to cleanse unarmed civilians, neither tanks nor artillery are necessary.

In order to secure Clark's first measure of merit to avoid losing aircraft, the Allies initially launched attacks against Serbia's IADs and Command and Control targets while neglecting FRY ground forces. For reasons discussed previously, the Allies never destroyed the FRY's IAD capability. By the third day of the campaign, General Short delayed the F-117 Stealth Fighter missions for lack of targets. After only two and half days of bombing, the Allies had exhausted the entire target list with no sign of capitulation by Milosevic.[153]

For numerous reasons, the target selection process was slow and difficult to say the least. NATO operated by consensus, by which each government reviewed and approved the selection of targets. The friction over target selection emerged in civilian versus military leadership and the U.S. and Britain in disagreement with France and Italy. Germany was reluctant to bomb Serbia given its history with the destruction of Belgrade in World War II.[154] This lack of consensus is symptomatic of "war among the people." U.S. Senator Gordon H. Smith remarked to the U.S. Senate Committee on Foreign Relations, "I was troubled…over the degree to which political considerations affected NATO's military strategy…even to the point where politicians… questioned and sometimes vetoed a target that had been selected by the military."[155]

---

[152]Ibid., 27-28, 30, 56.

[153]Halberstam, *War in a Time of Peace: Bush, Clinton and the Generals,* 451.

[154]Ibid., 452; Nardulli, et al., *Disjointed War: Military Operations in Kosovo, 1999,* 4-5.

[155]Gordon Smith, "The War in Kosovo and a Post War Analysis," U.S. Senate Committee on Foreign Relations, 106th Congress, 1st Session, October 6, 2000.

Clark increased military pressure on Milosevic beginning on 28 March, with a broader target set.[156] In early April, NATO began striking infrastructure in Serbia to include major bridges in Belgrade and the oil refinery at Panveco. General Clark simultaneously expanded the number of aircraft available to ratchet up pressure on Milosevic. On 9 April, he asked for eighty-two additional U.S. aircraft and again on 13 April, asked for another 300, bringing the total number of aircraft to approximately 800.[157] Despite the increased effort, NATO was largely unable to stop the ethnic cleansing and displacement of civilians from their homes.

TURNING POINT

The turning point for the Allies came about as they realized the concept of "fighting so as not to lose the force" by limiting the campaign to an air only option was failing to achieve the desired political solution in a timely manner. An air campaign, expected to last only a few days, was dragging on into weeks with no foreseeable end in sight. In addition, without the option or at least a threat of ground troops against Milosevic, the military strategy demonstrated a lack of understanding for the context of the campaign. Milosevic feared NATO ground units operating in Kosovo and especially in the FRY as evidenced by the rejection of the Rambouillet Peace Accord, which included such a clause. Consistent with Smith's theory, the determination to use both an air campaign coupled with ground forces had the potential to exponentially increase the utility of force and push Milosevic to peace talks.

The Allied bombing campaign continued into April with very little sign of Milosevic settling for peace and returning to negotiations. This realization finally strengthened and focused Allied resolve to prevail against Milosevic. As early as 9 April, Secretary General Javier Solana

---

[156]Nardulli, et al., *Disjointed War: Military Operations in Kosovo, 1999,* 32.

[157]Ibid., 32.

covertly gave General Clark permission to begin exploring ground operations in Kosovo.[158]

General Clark also pressed the issue with Secretary of Defense William Cohen, Secretary of

Defense and General Hugh Shelton.[159] The British also understood the necessity for a ground

campaign, which in their opinion, would give the operation a chance for success. Both the U.S.

and the British were looking at beginning a ground offensive in early to mid-September 1999.[160]

The timing of NATO's 50th Anniversary Summit offered the allies an opportunity to

evaluate the first month of military operations against Serbia and to determine a strategy to bring

Milosevic back to peace negotiations.[161] Very quickly, the agenda became loaded with the FRY's

stranglehold on Kosovo and specifically, countering Milosevic's stubbornness and failure to

accept Allied terms. Senior leaders and partners in NATO began to understand the struggle was

bigger than Kosovo; it was also about the purpose of NATO and its role in the post-Cold War

world. This was in fact the first conflict for NATO following the end of the Cold War, and in

mid-April the effectiveness of Operation ALLIED FORCE was far different from an expected

three-day air campaign and quick victory. During the summit, a North Atlantic Council (NAC)

member noted the challenge as follows and captured the spirit of NATO's new found resolve:

"The crisis in Kosovo represents a fundamental challenge to the value for which NATO has stood

since its foundation: democracy, human rights and the rule of law...We will not allow this

---

[158]Clark, *Waging Modern War*, 252.

[159]Ibid., 253-254.

[160]Nardulli, et al., *Disjointed War: Military Operations in Kosovo, 1999,* 40-41; The British Ministry of Defence began drawing up ground invasion plans in June 1998 with six different options including a full invastion of Serbia. Patrick Wintour and Peter Beaumont, "Revealed: The Secret Plan to Invade Kosovo," *The Guardian,* 17 July 1999, http://www.guardian.co.uk/world/1999/jul/18/balkans1 (accessed 9 March 2013).

[161]NATO held the 50th Anniversary Summit 23-24 April 1999, in Washington, DC; Nardulli, et al., *Disjointed War: Military Operations in Kosovo, 1999,* 36-37.

campaign of terror to succeed. NATO is determined to prevail."[162] Author Benjamin Lambeth

noted the summit was "pivotal in solidifying NATO's collective determination not to lose."[163]

Author David Halberstram noted that only in the face of failure did NATO find the

resolve to put forth the effort to win the conflict on NATO's terms. Ultimately, it was Prime

Minister Tony Blair and President Clinton who pushed the agenda of resolve and determination to

prevail against the FRY.[164] The Clinton administration had decided going into the summit the key

goal was to demonstrate Allied unity to Milosevic. Prime Minister Blair specifically pushed for

the start of planning to use ground forces in Kosovo and Serbia. They were both successful in

achieving their goals.[165] Following the summit, NATO authorized General Clark to plan for an

Allied ground phase. Simultaneously, NATO significantly expanded the air campaign's target list

and lifted bombing restrictions in downtown Belgrade.[166]

In Washington, Sandy Berger began to realize either the threat or actual employment of

ground forces in Kosovo could ultimately make the difference for the Allied effort. Beginning in

May, he composed a draft letter for President Clinton with three options that included the

following: arming the Kosovo Albanians, continuing the bombing campaign while waiting to

begin a ground offensive in the spring 2000, or, finally, to push hard for a ground invasion in

September 1999. The rationale behind a fall 1999 ground offensive was to ensure a favorable

---

[162]Heads of State and Government Participating in the Meeting of the North Atlantic Council in Washington, DC, 23-24 April 1999, "Statement on Kosovo," *NATO Press Release* S-1 (99)62, Washington, DC, 1999.

[163]Benjamin S. Lambeth, *NATO's Air War for Kosovo: A Strategic and Operational Assessment* (Santa Monica, CA: RAND, MR 1365-AF, 2001), 38.

[164]Halberstam, *War in a Time of Peace: Bush, Clinton and the Generals,* 470-471.

[165]Papacosma, Kay, and Rubin, *NATO After Fifty Years,* 16.

[166]Halberstam, *War in a Time of Peace: Bush, Clinton and the Generals,* 470-471.

military and political outcome prior to winter, allowing time for displaced personnel and refugees to find adequate shelter.[167]

On 18 May 1999, less than a month after the NATO summit, President Clinton announced, "All options are on the table," thus publically reversing his original policy of no ground troops in the FRY.[168] On 27 May, key NATO country leadership met formerly to discuss the use of ground troops. Countries in attendance at the meeting in Bonn, Germany, included the United States, Great Britain, France, Germany, and Italy.[169] The fruits of the NATO summit in terms of resolve and cohesion had begun to gain both traction and momentum.

Prior to the NATO meeting on 27 May, intelligence sources noted the air war was beginning to have a significant impact on Milosevic as demonstrated by the political isolation from his closest allies within Serbia. Milosevic began to act erratically and he noticeably reduced the number of his public appearances.[170] NATO demonstrated its new found resolve by increasing the intensity of the air campaign as the weather improved over Serbia and Kosovo in mid-May. As a result of better weather, Allied aircraft were now able to apply pressure by destroying Serb armored units while the KLA, numbering as many as 10,000 under arms, fought the Serbs on the ground and to a limited extent, drew them out of their hiding places. NATO's renewed efforts immediately increased the number of Serb Army desertions. Additionally, the threat of NATO ground troops in the FRY played a significant role in the desertions as well.[171]

---

[167]Daalder and O'Hanlon, *Winning Ugly, NATO's War to Save Kosovo,* 158-160.

[168]William Jefferson Clinton, President, "Remarks Prior to Discussions With King Abdullah II of Jordan and an Exchange With Reporters." Washington, DC, May 18, 1999, http://www.presidency.ucsb.edu/ws/index.php?pid=57589&st =kosovo&st1=.

[169]Ibid., 495.

[170]Ibid., 472.

[171]Ibid., 472-473.

<u>Capitulation and Aftermath</u>

Several authors have put forward different rationale explaining why Milosevic did surrender in early June 1999. Although it is an over simplification to cite one particular aspect as the sole reason for capitulation, the increasing intensity of the air war played a major role. Additionally, the new planning for the use of ground forces probably shaped Milosevic's decision to surrender. The U.S. Army had already established a foothold on the continent with Task Force HAWK.[172] The direct cause for these new developments however was the Allies' newly demonstrated resolve following NATO's 50th Anniversary summit, which finally gave the military campaign utility. Milosevic's hopes to destroy alliance cohesion had failed and in fact, had the opposite effect as key NATO nations supported the use of ground troops following the conclusion of the summit.

Another critical factor in Milosevic's capitulation was the loss of support from Russia.[173] Due to intense internal politics and a newly formed fragile government, Russian President Boris Yeltsin could not stand by idly while NATO bombed the FRY.[174] His hopes were for a quick conclusion to NATO military operations. When that did not happen, Yeltsin incrementally began to pressure Milosevic to come to terms with NATO. His efforts culminated when he appointed Viktor Chernomyrdin, a former Russian Prime Minister, as part of a special envoy team to deal directly with Milosevic. The President of Finland Marti Ahtisaari and U.S. Deputy Secretary of

---

[172]Nardulli, et al., *Disjointed War: Military Operations in Kosovo*, 41, 44-45.

[173]Daalder and O'Hanlon, *Winning Ugly, NATO's War to Save Kosovo,* 5.

[174]According to Jim Nichol, Russia opposed NATO's air campaign against Serbia for several reasons: Russians appeared sympathetic toward their "fellow" Orthodox Christian Serbs and believed it was in Serbia's sovereign rights as a nation to quell what Russian Foreign Minister Ivanov labeled a "breeding ground for Islamic extremism" (1); 92% of Russians disapproved NATO's air campaign against Serbia (2); NATO actions appeared to threaten Yeltsin's authority, highlighting Russia's overall weakness in the region (4); some believed the campaign was fought under the auspice of NATO enlargement and Russia would be next (5); U.S. Library of Congress, Congressional Research Service, *Kosovo Conflict: Russian Responses and Implications for the United States.*

State Strobe Talbott, who served as a NATO representative, were also on the team.[175] The delegation made it clear to Milosevic they had not come to negotiate with him, but instead to dictate the terms for his surrender. After Ahtisaari explained the terms of the settlement, Milosevic turned for help from Viktor Chernomyrdin, who offered none. Quickly, Milosevic realized Russia was now on board with NATO and continued resistance was futile.[176]

On 9 June 1999, NATO's Lieutenant General Michael Short and Yugoslav General Svetozar Marjanovic signed the Military Technical Agreement (MTA).[177] The next day, per Solana's instruction to General Clark, NATO's air campaign ended.[178] The MTA called for a phased withdrawal of Serb forces coincident with the arrival of UN ground forces to monitor the return of refugees. UNSCR 1244 authorized the deployment of an international peacekeeping force in Kosovo. Serb forces withdrew from Kosovo in less than eleven days in compliance with the MTA. Additionally, a buffer zone was set up on Kosovo's northern border with Serbia, extending three miles into Serbia.[179]

Although the West did achieve a settlement for Kosovo, according to author Misha Glenny, the "claim to a moral victory in the Balkans…was unsurprising but irrelevant, within the larger historical context of the relations between the great powers and the Balkans." The West had intervened in the Balkans on many occasions throughout history, never truly reversing the trend of conflict in the region. Glenny's statement is another testament to General Smith's war among the people which holds, "conflicts tend to be timeless." Going back to the late 1800s,

---

[175]Ibid., 476-477.

[176]Nardulli, et al., *Disjointed War: Military Operations in Kosovo,* 43.

[177]For more information regarding the Military Technical Agreement, see NATO's webpage on the organization's involvement on Kosovo titled, Military Technical Agreement; NATO, "Military Technical Agreement," http://www.nato.int/kosovo/docu/a990609a.htm (accessed 9 April 2013).

[178]Daalder and O'Hanlon, *Winning Ugly, NATO's War to Save Kosovo*, 233.

[179]Nardulli, et al., *Disjointed War: Military Operations in Kosovo,* 44, 99-101.

Western powers replaced the Ottoman Empire with alliances on the Balkan peninsula. The second intervention came to fruition in 1923 following the Treaty of Lausanne and the largely disruptive population exchange between Turkey and Greece. Both countries are still in conflict today, requiring the persistent deployment of UN peacekeepers on the island of Cyprus. In the third instance, Italy attacked Greece during World War II followed by the Soviet's occupation of the Balkans behind the "Iron Curtain." Finally, war in Bosnia in the early 1990s rounds out the four interventions in the Balkans in just a little over a one hundred year period.[180] Unlike the Bosnian Dayton Accords however, the Kosovo "peace" agreement did not provide a political settlement as it failed to address Kosovo's independence. Although Kosovo declared its independence from Serbia in 2008, not all nations recognize Kosovo's independence, most notably, Serbia.[181]

As a result of the conflict, financial losses to Serbia, Kosovo, and the surrounding region, as well as the costs associated with reconstruction in the FRY, amounts to astounding figures. Economic losses suffered in Serbia and Kosovo ranged from $7-10 billion. Reconstruction in both countries cost another $10 billion, spent over a three-to-five year period. Other countries in the Balkans experienced a short-term drop in their Gross Domestic Product (GDP) as well. The worst hit, Macedonia and Bosnia-Herzegovina have lost an estimated 5 percent of GDP while Romania and Hungary may have lost as little as 0.5 percent. Additionally, following the end of hostilities, the Vienna Institute of Economics estimated "stability" in the Balkans would cost $100 billion.[182]

Events in Kosovo support Smith's theory of "war among the people." Initially, NATO failed to state clear political end states for Kosovo and the Balkans. Leading up to the campaign, it was difficult for NATO military leadership to determine the appropriate strategy that would

---

[180]Glenny, *The Balkans: Nationalism, War and the Great Powers, 1804-1999*, 661.

[181]Nardulli, et al., *Disjointed War: Military Operations in Kosovo, 199*, 109.

[182]Glenny, *The Balkans: Nationalism, War and the Great Powers, 1804-1999*, 660.

maximize the utility of force. Forcing Milosevic back to the negotiation table through bombing, while maintaining alliance cohesion and preservation of life (for civilians and NATO pilots), hardly translated to a military strategy.[183] Additionally, the U.S. decision to publically rule out the use of ground forces well before the campaign began, given internal politics and public opinion, certainly affected Milosevic's calculus for the West's commitment to action in Kosovo. Finally, the utility of alliance warfare raises questions as the United States must decide if it will continue with war by consensus at the risk of sacrificing military efficiency and effectiveness.[184]

In the author's opinion, Smith's "war among the people" theory is by definition an incremental military approach, allowing time for diplomatic maneuvering while simultaneously intensifying military operations. The difference with Kosovo and the proper application of Smith's theory however, was NATO's inability to set clear political goals prior to commencing military operations, something Smith specifically warns against as one of his fundamental beliefs.[185] The pressure to "fight so as not to lose the force," also led NATO and the U.S. to rule out ground forces many months before dropping the first bombs. In the author's opinion, this also explains the restrictive rules of engagement imposed on NATO pilots to both minimize collateral damage and the possibility of losing pilots and their aircraft to Serb Integrated Air Defenses and manpads.

In the context of the campaign's strategic goals, the destruction of Serbian equipment and forces is unknown. Although no count of equipment coming out of Kosovo was made, the Serb redeploying units appeared both combat effective and with high morale.[186] In a fall 1999 NATO press conference, General Clark stated, "We never thought we'd destroyed even half what was

---

[183]Herspring, *The Pentagon and the Presidency,* 372.

[184]Papacosma, Kay, and Rubin, *NATO After Fifty Years,* 21.

[185]Smith, *The Utility of Force: the Art of War in the Modern World,* 21.

[186]Nardulli, et al., *Disjointed War: Military Operations in Kosovo, 1999,* 4.

there."[187] At the very least however, the air campaign forced Serb ground units to hide their large equipment, rendering them unusable against the Albanian Kosovars and the KLA.

Estimates from Ambassador Daalder and O'Hanlon claim that up to 10,000 people, mainly civilians, were killed by Serb ground units and approximately 800,000 people were forced to leave Kosovo and another 100,000 were relocated somewhere in Kosovo away from their homes.[188] Eventually, nearly all of the ethnic Albanians were able to return to their homes within just a few weeks of the cessation of combat. All Serb forces left Kosovo as agreed upon in the Military Technical Agreement while the U.N. simultaneously inserted a peacekeeping force. Additionally, an international administration was setup to run the Kosovar government, successfully excluding Serbia from governance in Kosovo and involvement in their political affairs.[189]

CONCLUSION

But Kosovo also reminded us that any time a nation considers the use of force it has to ask a number of questions, such as whether the lives of its citizens and the security of its nation or the fundamental principles of its people are directly threatened; whether the vital interests of its closest allies are jeopardized, risking the stability on which that nation's way of life depends; whether the wheel of conflict, if allowed to spin on its violent axis, will draw other nations into its vortex at greater and more devastating cost and; whether inaction threatens humanitarian catastrophe or establishes a precedent of allowing unfettered criminal behavior to undermine international peace and stability. [190]

Barring the outbreak of industrial world war, former Secretary of Defense, William Cohen's comment in the wake of the Allied air campaign over Kosovo reflects the essence of

---

[187]Wesley K. Clark, General (USA) and John D. W. Corley, Brigadier General (USAF), Press Conference on the Kosovo Strike Assessment (Headquarters, Supreme Allied Command Europe, Mons, Belgium, 16 September 1999).

[188]Daalder and O'Hanlon, *Winning Ugly, NATO's War to Save Kosovo,* 3.

[189]Ibid., 4.

[190]William S. Cohen, speech given to the International Institute for Strategic Studies, Hotel Del Coronado, San Diego, 9 September 1999, CA, http://www.defense.gov/speeches/speech.aspx? speechid=470, (accessed 27 September 2012).

General Smith's war among the people. This new paradigm of war among the people clearly fits the Kosovo military campaign and offers useful incites regarding future 21st century warfare for those who are interested in advancing their understanding of the profession of arms. NATO's combat operations against the FRY were the third conflict since the end of the Cold War (first Gulf War and conflict in Bosnia). Following the end of hostilities, leaders in both Iraq and the FRY remained in power as the Allies had achieved their limited objective for each campaign without their removal.

Since maintaining alliance cohesion was one of them main NATO objectives, the alliance created restrictive ROE for NATO targeteers and pilots. The ROE aimed to prevent civilian collateral damage and in general, NATO succeeded at this goal. Additionally, NATO feared the loss of aircraft and NATO pilots would constitute significant challenges for on-going military operations. Although an American F-117 Stealth Fighter was shot down, American combat rescue forces quickly rescued the downed pilot. In fact, the campaign did not begin until search and rescue capabilities were in theater and fully operational. All of these restraints were developed out of NATO's fear that a catastrophic event would unravel the alliance. Given the action of key NATO nations throughout the campaign, the concern was legitimate and subsequent actions to mitigate the risk are consistent with fighting "war among the people."

At the very onset of the international community's recognition of trouble in the Balkans, the United States ruled out the use of ground forces. Leading up to NATO's military campaign, President Clinton estimated Congress and the American people would never accept the use of U.S. ground forces in the FRY and if they did, even the President himself was reluctant to commit a large number of forces. Unfortunately, his public statements to that effect, instantly ceded the initiative to Milosevic. Additionally, NATO was unable to come up with clear political objectives prior to the beginning of the campaign. As a result, NATO military leadership was not able to develop a military strategy with clear end states. Nine days into the bombing campaign, General

Clark held VTCs with his senior General Officers to determine military metrics and the political end states NATO was seeking.[191] This lack of clear political objectives continued to haunt the Allies until NATO's 50th Anniversary Summit in the latter part of April 1999, almost a full month after military operations commenced over the FRY.

Unfortunately, Western leadership failed to address the crux of the political settlement, an independent Kosovo. Even though Kosovo declared its independence from Serbia in 2008, to this day, NATO maintains a peace force in the country. The political agreement also failed to address the peaceful coexistence of Serbs and ethnic Albanians in Kosovo as the Albanian Kosovars quickly moved to forcefully expel Serbs from Kosovo as soon as all Serb military forces left the country. In spite of these setbacks however, the military campaign ultimately succeeded since it set the condition for a political settlement. Consistent with Smith's war among the people, conflict in Kosovo and in the Balkans region is timeless and will continue to span generations as it has for centuries.

General Smith's theory and his six characteristics that underpin it, provide key considerations and lessons learned from previous conflicts. Military and political leaders need to heed the lessons of the incremental war fought in Kosovo and understand Smith's characteristics that describe this new paradigm of war. General Smith also warns against the catastrophic mistake of failing to establish a clear link between the political end state and the military strategy used to achieve it. At the beginning of military operations in Kosovo, a strategy had not been clearly articulated and military action was taken out of the need "to do something," using the air campaign over Bosnia as the template for action. As witnessed by Milosevic's failure to capitulate after three days of bombing as originally anticipated, the initial campaign proved military action lacked utility as Belgrade merely dug in and weathered NATO bombings. Finally,

---

[191]Clark, *Waging Modern War*, 233.

a political end state was developed and articulated following NATO's 50th Anniversary held at the end of April 1999. Even more important was the Allies' newly fashioned will and determination to expand air operations and the beginning of plans to deploy ground forces.

In order to resolve this lack of coherence between political and military objective, creators of U.S. doctrine need to change the framework from which military and political leaders interact and instead use a four-tiered level of war model, similar to the model proposed by General Smith.[192] As background and to gain appreciation for this new way of thinking, Clausewitz recognized two tiers, namely the tactical and strategic level whereas Edward Luttwack recognized five and current U.S. military doctrine supports three levels.[193] All three models begin with the lowest level, building up toward the strategic level. The difference with Smith's model is it formerly recognizes the political aspect as its own distinct level, with the four levels in the following order: political, strategic, theater, and tactical. By recognizing the political level first, military conflict begins with a political aim. The political level in this model provides both a source of power and guidance for the next three levels. Additionally, civilian leadership, at least in most Western nations, is at the apex of military command.

Both politicians and military leaders at all levels need to understand and appreciate this new paradigm of 21st century warfare and more importantly, plan for it. Unlike in Kosovo, nations and alliances must develop clear political end states directly linked to the military means prior to beginning military action. When possible, leaders should act and speak so as not to rule out any particular military option as the use or even threat of a particular military capability may

---

[192]Smith, *The Utility of Force: the Art of War in the Modern World,* 12.

[193]Clausewitz, *On War,* 128; In his book *Strategy, the Logic of War and Peace,* Luttwak proposes five levels of strategy: technical, tactical, operational, theater and grand strategy. The technical level focuses on the tools of warfare, the specific weapon systems and the interplay with the forces using them. Theater is introduced to tie together the various operational levels which Luttwak portends are autonomous (87-91); Joint Publication 3-0, *Joint Operations,* glossary 14, 16, 17.

be enough to coerce a settlement. The power of the press in war among the people is immense, as demonstrated by the campaign in Kosovo. Additionally, military commanders need to understand the limited, constrained, and even incremental application of military action when conducting war among the people. Although the preference is for full-scale high intensity conflict, war among the people is not about fighting the preferred military way of conflict, but instead aimed at setting the conditions for a limited political settlement. In fact, unconstrained warfare in the 21st century can destroy an alliance and the international community's support for military action. In the context of General Smith's war among the people, the application of absolute and unconstrained force will most likely result in a quick end to military operations and complete failure to obtain political objectives. Although perceived as slow and incremental, the deliberate application and increasing pressure of military power against the FRY, in conjunction with factors discussed previously, succeeded in bringing Milosevic to the bargaining table.

APPENDIX 1: KEY PERSONNEL[194]

Abbott, Steve. Admiral, U.S.Navy; Deputy Commander in Chief, U.S. European Command.

Albright, Madeleine. U.S. Secretary of State.

Berger, Samuel R. "Sandy." National Security Adviser to the U.S. President.

Blair, Tony. Prime Minister, United Kingdom.

Casey, George. BG, USA; Deputy Director, Strategic Plans and Policy (J-5), The Joint Staff.

Chirac, Jacques. President, France.

Clinton,William J. President of the United States.

Cohen, William S. U.S. Secretary of Defense.

Ellis, James. Admiral, U.S. Navy; Commander-in-Chief, Allied Forces Southern Europe;

 Commander-in-Chief, U.S. Naval Forces, Europe.

Hill, Christopher. U.S. Ambassador to Macedonia.

Holbrooke, Richard C. Consultant to the Dept of State; U.S. Ambassador to the United Nations.

Johnson, Jay. Admiral, U.S. Navy; Chief of Naval Operations.

Jumper, John. General, U.S. Air Force; Commanding General, U.S. Air Forces, Europe.

Meigs, Montgomery. General, U.S. Army; Commanding General, U.S. Army Europe.

Naumann, Klaus. General, German Army; Chairman of the NATO Military Committee.

Ralston, Joseph. General, U.S. Air Force; Vice Chairman, Joint Chiefs of Staff.

Reimer, Dennis. General, U.S Army; U.S. Army Chief of Staff.

Ryan, Michael. General, U.S. Air Force, U.S. Air Force Chief of Staff.

Scalfaro, Oscar. President, Italy.

Schroeder, Gerhard. Chancellor,Germany.

Shelton, Henry "Hugh". General, U.S. Army; Chairman, Joint Chiefs of Staff.

---

[194]Clark, *Waging Modern War,* ix-xiii.

Short, Michael. Lieut Gen, USAF; Commander, Air Forces Southern Europe, U.S. 16th Air Force.

Simitis, Konstantinos. Prime Minister, Greece.

Smith, Rupert. General, U.K.Army; Deputy Supreme Allied Commander, Europe.

Solana, Javier. Secretary General, North Atlantic Treaty Organization.

Talbott, Strobe. U.S. Deputy Secretary of State.

Veshbow, Alexander "Sandy". U.S. Ambassador to NATO.

Yeltsin, Boris. President, Russia.

APPENDIX 2: MAP OF KOSOVO[195]

[195]*The World Factbook*, Central Intelligence Agency,
https://www.cia.gov/library/publications/the-world-factbook/docs/refmaps.html (Accessed 9
April 2013.

[196]Air South Command briefing (Vicenza, Italy) presented to Air University, Air War College, Maxwell AFB, Alabama, 23 October 1999, http://www.airpower.maxwell.af.mil/airchronicles/apj/apj00/fal00/strickland.htm (accessed 9 April 2013).

BIBLIOGRAPHY

Memoirs and Primary Sources

Albright, Madeleine with Bill Woodward. *Madeleine Albright, Madam Secretary*. New York: Miramax Books, 2003.

Albright, Madeleine, Secretary of State. "U.S. and NATO Policy Toward the Crisis in Kosovo." Statement before the Senate Foriegn Relations Committee, 20 April 1999. http://www2.lhric.org/validation/war/articles/albright.html (accessed 19 November 2012).

_____. "Press Briefing at the Ministry of Foreign Affairs." Rome: U.S. Department of State, 7 March 1998.

Air South Command briefing (Vicenza, Italy) presented to Air University, Air War College, Maxwell AFB, Alabama, 23 October 1999, http://www.airpower.maxwell.af.mil/airchronicles/apj/apj00/fal00/strickland.htm (accessed 9 April 2013).

Blair, Tony. *A Journey: My Political Life*. New York: A. Knopf, 2010.

Clark, Wesley K. *Waging Modern War*. New York: Public Affairs, 2001.

Clinton Presidential Records Mandatory Declassification Review, An Administrative marker used by the William J. Clinton Presidential Library Staff, 200 pages.

Clinton, William J. *My Life*. New York: Alfred A.Knopf, 2004.

_____. Interview by Dan Rather, Columbia Broadcasting System, 31 March 1999.

_____. President. "Address to the Nation on Airstrikes Against Serbian Targets in the Federal Republic of Yugoslavia (Serbia and Montenegro)." Washington, DC, 24 March 1999. http://www.presidency.ucsb.edu/ws/?pid=57305.

_____. President. "Remarks Prior to Discussions With King Abdullah II of Jordan and an Exchange With Reporters." Washington, DC, May 18, 1999. http://www.presidency.ucsb.edu/ws/index.php?pid=57589&st =kosovo&st1=.

Department of Defense. "News Briefing." Statement by Kenneth Bacon, Assistant Secretary of Defense for Public Affairs. Washington DC, 23 March 1999.

_____. "News Briefing." Statement by Kenneth Bacon, Assistant Secretary of Defense for Public Affairs. Washington, DC, 27 March 1999.

_____. *Kosovo/Operation Allied Force Report After-Action Report to Congress*. Washington, DC: Government Printing Office, 31 January 2000.

Heads of State and Government Participating in the Meeting of the North Atlantic Council in Washington, DC, April 23 and 24, 1999. "Statement on Kosovo." *NATO Press Release S-1 (99)62*. Washington, DC, 1999.

Shelton, Henry H. *Without Hesitation: The Odyssey of an American Warrior*. New York: St. Martin's Press, 2010.

Solana, Javier Secretary General of NATO. "Press Release (1999)040." *NATO Information*. 23 March 1999. http://www.nato.inf/docu.pr.1999/p99-040e.htm (accessed 21 June 2012).

Secondary Sources

Boot, Max. "The New American Way of War." *Foreign Affairs* 82, no. 4 (July/August 2003): 41-58.

Brookings Institute. http://www.brookings.edu/experts/ohanlonm (accessed 28 November 2012).

Byman, Jeremy. *Madam Secretary: The Story of Madeleine Albright*. Greensboro, NC: Morgan Reynolds , 2008. EBSCO Host, Combined Arms Research Library Internet Site, (accessed 26 September 2012).

Carlson, Ingvar and Shridath Ramphal. "NATO's Vigilante Warfare gives a Bad Example to the World." *International Herald Tribune* (1 April 1999).

Cavendish, Richard. "Tito Elected President of the Former Republic of Yugoslavia." *History Today* 52, no. 1 (June 2003).

Chairman, Joint Chiefs of Staff. Joint Publication (JP) 3-0, *Joint Operations*. Washington, DC: Government Printing Office, 2011.

Charter of the United Nations. http://www.un.org/en/documents/charter/chapter7.shtml, (accessed on 30 September 2012).

Clark, Wesley K., General (USA) and Brigadier General (USAF) John D. W. Corley. Press Conference on the Kosovo Strike Assessment. Mons, Belgium: Headquarters, Supreme Allied Command Europe (16 September 1999).

Clarke, Michael. "Airpower, Force and Coercion." *The Dynamics of Airpower*. Edited by Andrew Lambert and Arthur C. Williamson. Bracknell, U.K.: Her Majesty's Stationary Office, 1996.

Clausewitz, Carl Von. *On War*. Edited and translated by Michael Howard and Peter Paret. Princeton, NJ: Princeton University Press, 1976.

Cohen, Eliot A. *Soldiers, Statesmen, and Leadership in Wartime: Supreme Command*. New York: Anchor Books, 2003.

Cohen, Michael A. "The Powell Doctrine's Enduring Relevance." *World Politics Review*, 22 July 2009. http://www.worldpoliticsreview.com/articles/4100/the-powell-doctrines-enduring-relevanc (accessed 29 January 2013).

Cohen, William S. Interview by PBS Frontline (n.d.). http://www.pbs.org/wgbh/pages/frontline/ shows/kosovo/interviews/cohen.html (accessed 29 January 2013).

_____. Speech, International Institute for Strategic Studies, Hotel del Coronado, San Diego, CA. 9 September 1999. http://www.defense.gov/speeches/speech.aspx?speechid=470 (accessed 27 September 2012).

_____. Biographical Directory of the United States Congress. http://bioguide.congress.gov/ scripts/biodisplay.pl?index=C000598 (accessed 29 Janaury 2013).

Cordesman, Anthony. *The Lessons and Non-Lessons of the Air and Missile Campaign in Kosovo*. Westport, CT: Praeger, 2001.

Daalder, Ivo. Interviewed by PBS Frontline. n.d.

_____. Statement to U.S. Senate Foreign Relations Committee, 22 April 2009. http://nato.usmission.gov/mission/ambassador.html (accessed 17 November 2012).

Daalder, Ivo H. and Michael E. O'Hanlon. *Winning Ugly, NATO's War to Save Kosovo.* Washington, DC: Brookings Institution Press, 2000.

Defence Committee. Fourteenth Report, Report to Parliament. London: Her Majesty's Stationery Office, 1999. http://www.parliament.the-stationery-office.co.uk/pa/ cm199900/cmselect/cmdfence /347/34702.htm (accessed 21 June 2012).

Dennis Drew. "Rolling Thunder 1965: Anatomy of a Failure." Air University, School of Advanced Airpower Studies. Maxwell Air Force Base, Air University Press, October 1986. http://www.au.af.mil/au/awc/awcgate/readings/drew2.htm (accessed 9 March 2013).

Fitchett, Joseph. "Main Winner: U.S. Support for EU." *International Herald Tribune* (11 June 1999).

Glenny, Misha. *The Balkans: Nationalism, War and the Great Powers, 1804-1999.* New York: Penguin, 2001.

Graham, Bradley. "Joint Chiefs Doubted Air Strategy." *Washington Post,* 5 April 1999.

Gray, Colin S. *Another Bloody Century, Future Warfare.* Phoeniz, AZ: Orion Books, 2005.

Halberstam, David. *War in a Time of Peace: Bush, Clinton and the Generals.* New York: Scribner's, 2000.

Henriksen, Dag. *NATO's Gamble: Combining Diplomacy and Airpower in the Kosovo Crisis 1998-1999.* Annapolis, MD: Naval Institute Press, 2007.

Herspring, Dale R. *The Pentagon and the Presidency.* Wichita, KS: University Press of Kansas, 2005.

Holbrooke, Richard. *To End a War.* New York: The Modern Library, 1998.

Judah, Tim. *Kosovo: War and Revenge.* New Haven: Yale University Press, 2000.

Kaplan, Robert D. *Balkan Ghosts: A Journey Through History.* New York: St. Martin's Press, 1993.

Kitfield, James. "Not so Sacred Borders." *PBS Frontline,* 2000. http://www.pbs.org/wgbh/pages/ frontline/shows/kosovo/procon/kitfield.html, (accessed on 28 January 2013).

Kosovo Country Review. Country Watch, Inc. http://connection.ebscohost.com 2012, (accessed 27 January 2013).

Kozaryn, Linda D. "NATO Orders Air Strikes to End 'Humanitarian Catastrophe.'" *Armed Forces Press Service*, 24 March 1999. http://www.defense.gov/News/ NewsArticle.aspx?ID=42000, (accessed 28 January 2013).

Kuhn, Thomas S. *Structure of Scientific Revolutions*, 3rd ed. London and Chicago: University of Chicago Press, 1996.

Lambeth, Banjamin S. *NATO's Air War for Kosovo: A Strategic and Operational Assessment.* Santa Monica, CA: RAND, MR 1365-AF, 2001.

Luttwak, Edward N. *Strategy: The Logic of War and Peace.* Cambridge, MA; London, England: The Belknap Press of Harvard University Press, 2003.

Nardulli, Bruce R., Walter L. Perry, Brice Prinie, John Gordon IV, and John G. McGinn. *Disjointed War: Military Operations in Kosovo, 1999.* Santa Monica, CA; Arlington, VA; Pittsburgh, PA: RAND, 2002.

61

Nation, R. Craig. *War in the Balkans, 1991-2002.* Carlisle Barracks, Carlisle, PA: Strategic Studies Institute, U.S. Army War College, August 2003.

NATO. "Political and Military Objectives of NATO Action with Regard to the Crisis in Kosovo." *NATO Information,* 23 March 1999. http://www.nato.inf/docu.pr.1999/p99-043e.htm (accessed 21 June 2012).

_____. http://www.nato.int/cps/en/natolive/topics_49763.html (accessed 28 November 2012).

_____. http://www.nato.int/cps/en/natolive/news_69290.htm (accessed 8 April 2013).

_____. http://www.nato.int/kosovo/docu/a990609a.htm (accessed 9 April 2013).

Naumann, Klaus. Interviewed by PBS Frontline. 2000.

Papacosma, Victor S., Sean Kay, Mark R. Rubin, eds. *NATO After Fifty Years.* Wilmington, DE: Scholarly Resources, 2001.

Patney, Vinod. "Air War in Kosovo." *Air Power Journal* 1, no. 1. Centre for Air Power Studies (Monsoon: 2004).

Priest, Dana. "Army's Apache Helicopter Rendered Impotent in Kosovo." *Washington Post,* 29 December 1999.

Roberson, Agneza Bozic. "The Role of Rhetoric in the Politicization of Ethnicity: Milosevic and the Yugoslav Ethnopolitical Conflict." *Razprve in Gradivo - Treaties & Documents*, no. 52 (2007).

Rothkopf, David J. *Running the World: The Inside Story of the National Security Council and the Architects of American Power.* New York: Public Affairs, 2005.

Ryan, Michael E, General (USAF). *The Air War over Serbia.* Ramstein Air Force Base, Germany: Studies and Analysis Directorate, United States Air Force in Europe, 2000.

Schelling, Thomas C. *Arms and Influence.* New Haven, CT: Yale University Press, 1966.

Short, Michael, Lieutenant General USAF. Interviewed by PBS Frontline. 22 February 2000.

Smith, Gordon. "The War in Kosovo and a Post War Analysis." US Senate Committee on Foreign Relations, 106th Congress, 1st Session, 6 October 2000.

Smith, R. Jeffrey. "Accord on Kosovo Remains Elusive." *Washington Post*, 12 October1998.

Smith, Rupert. *The Utility of Force: the Art of War in the Modern World.* New York: Vintage, 2008.

Stout, David. "U.S. General Who Led NATO to Retire Ahead of Schedule." *New York Times.* Ebscohost.com (accessed 27 September 2012).

Todorova, Maria. *Imagining the Balkans.* New York: Oxford, 1997.

U.S. Library of Congress. Congressional Research Service. *Kosovo Conflict: Russian Responses and Implications for the United States* by Jim Nichol. CRS Report RL30130. Washington, DC: Office of Congressional Information and Publishing, 2 June 1999.

_____. Congressional Research Service, *Kosovo: Lessons Learned from Operation Allied Force* by Paul E. Gallis. CRS Report RL30374. Washington, DC: Office of Congressional Information and Publishing, 19 November 1999.

_____. Congressional Research Service. *Kosovo: U.S. and Allied Military Operations*, by Steve Bowman, CRS Report 1B10027. Washington, DC: Office of Congressional Information and Publishing, 24 July 2000.

Vladisavljevic, Nebojsa. "Grassroots Groups, Milosevic or Dissident Intellectuals? A Controversy over the Orgins and Dynamics of the Mobilisation of Kosovo Serbs in the 1990s." *Nationalities Papers* 32, no. 4, (December 2004).

Weigley, Russell F. *The American Way of War: A History of United States Military Strategy and Policy*. Bloomington, IN: Indiana University Press, 1973.

Wintour, Peter and Peter Beaumont. "Revelaed: The Secret Plan to Invade Kosovo." *The Guardian*, 17 July 1999. http://www.guardian.co.uk/world/1999/jul/18/balkans1 (accessed 9 March 2013).

www.ingramcontent.com/pod-product-compliance
Lightning Source LLC
Chambersburg PA
CBHW081856280526
45789CB00007B/2724